JARRIT SMITH'S
1751
NEWCOMEN ENGINE

Steve Grudgings

© Steve Grudgings and
South Gloucestershire Mines Research Group 2012
Designed by Ian Pope
British Library Cataloguing-in-Publication Data. A catalogue record for
this book is available from the British Library
ISBN 13: 9780957233119

Printed and bound by Berforts Information Press, Eynsham, Oxfordshire
www.informationpress.com

This book is dedicated to my wife Diane and our children Nick, Mark, Sam and Els.

ACKNOWLEDGEMENTS

There are many individuals who have assisted in the production of this book and I would particularly like to thank David Cranstone, Chair of the Historical Metallurgy Society for guiding me through this specialist area. I am grateful to Geoff Hayes, President of the International Stationary Steam Engine Society for all his contributions, particularly those resulting from his involvement with the restoration of the 1811 Caprington Colliery Newcomen Engine now in Edinburgh museum. Ben Russell, Curator of Mechanical Engineering at the Science Museum and his colleagues have helped on a number of fronts, including allowing access to sections of the 1791 Pentrich engine normally out of bounds. Alan Bates organised detailed examination of the 1795 Elsecar Engine, John Powell kindly provided a number of illustrations from the Ironbridge Library. In addition to providing the information on John Wise's early Newcomen Engines in Bristol, Peter Tymków has also been able to shed light on the meaning of some of the more obscure words used in the bills.

Within the South Gloucestershire Mines Research Group (SGMRG) my particular thanks go to Ken Kemp for his diligent proof reading and generally keeping me on track. I also owe a debt of gratitude to all the team who work on the Serridge Engine excavation and conservation.

The permission of the Science Museum, Wiltshire & Swindon History Centre, Bristol Records Office, the University of Nottingham Manuscripts & Special Collections, Ironbridge Gorge Trust and Peter Berg to reproduce their materials are all gratefully acknowledged.

Finally, my thanks to Ian Pope for laying out and organising the printing of this book.

I would welcome any comments, observations or information to me at the address below.

Steve Grudgings April 2012
31, Laverstoke Lane, Laverstoke,
Whitchurch,Hampshire, RG287NY

INTRODUCTION

Whilst this account has been four years in the making, I am pleased that this has resulted in its publication in the year of the 300th anniversary of the installation of Thomas Newcomen's first engine. The catalyst for this book was the authors realisation that he had a full set of suppliers bills for the 1751 engine and after transcribing and researching them that there was a full story to be told. Good quality images of Newcomen Engines of this period are rare and no apology is made for the extensive use of photographs of the 1791 Pentrich Engine taken by Mr Anderson prior to its transfer to the Science Museum.

The author's rationale for producing a book of this size on a single engine was prompted by the insight these bills gives on how such engines were constructed an attempt has been made to set this out as clearly as possible. The author makes no claims that my assumptions on building methods are completely accurate but they have been derived as carefully as possible. Throughout images of components and contemporary processes, where relevant, are included to bring the text to life.

This engine, like its contemporaries was a bespoke product of self taught artisans who may not have been able to read or write and certainly will not have featured in the accounts of the great engineers. All of the author's research into colliery engineering points to the bulk of achievements being made by the unsung pit engineer or travelling engine wright. A few men (Newcomen and George Stephenson being the most obvious examples) have achieved fame through this route but are very much the exception. What has also become clear is how much knowledge relating to engine building has been lost, for example, no accounts of how boiler plates were cut, shaped and assembled could be found, nor any describing how an engine beam was constructed.

During the course of his research, the author has been part of the team that photographed and surveyed what is believed to be the United Kingdom's earliest complete Newcomen Engine house at Brislington (built c.1739) At the same time he has also been part of the small team uncovering and conserving the substantive remains of the 1791 Serridge Newcomen Engine, 300 yards from the site of the 1751 engine. One of the challenges in constructing this account, has been to know where to draw the boundaries between explaining the context and background for a specific aspect of the engines construction and providing excessive details of a particular facet. It is left to the reader to judge as to how well the balance has been struck.

PREFACE

The purpose of this account is to set out, for what is believed to be the first time, the sequence, materials, methods and operational context for the construction and commissioning of an early Newcomen 'atmospheric' pumping engine at Coalpit Heath (NGR ST676803) in South Gloucestershire in 1751. It is based on the surviving bills from the suppliers (thought to be a complete set) and supported by contemporary maps and related archival materials, specifically component illustrations.

The survival of a complete set of supplier's bills for an early Newcomen pumping engine is unusual if not unique. They are held in two different archives and are not thought to have been examined together before. This account seeks to explain how the engine was built based on the contents of these bills and their relationship with each other; it also draws on a range of related materials for which references are given.

The author suggests that this account deserves the reader's attention on the basis that it clarifies the processes, costs and timescales of commissioning of what was then state of the art technology clear to the point of being able to identify (in some cases) the day specific activities took place.

Broad peer review has been sought prior to publication but responsibility for errors is the authors alone.

The structure of this book is as follows:

Chapter 1   Sets out the overall historical, industrial, technical and local context.

Chapter 2   Sets out the detailed sequence of building and commissioning the engine.

Chapter 3   Looks at the bills in detail. Providing interpretation and technical information and examines what is known of the suppliers.

Chapter 4   Examines what we can conclude and what is of particular note.

Appendix 1   is a selected bibliography

Appendix 2   outlines what is known of the Palmer family of Engine Wrights

Appendix 3   lists other information sources for Newcomen Engine costs.

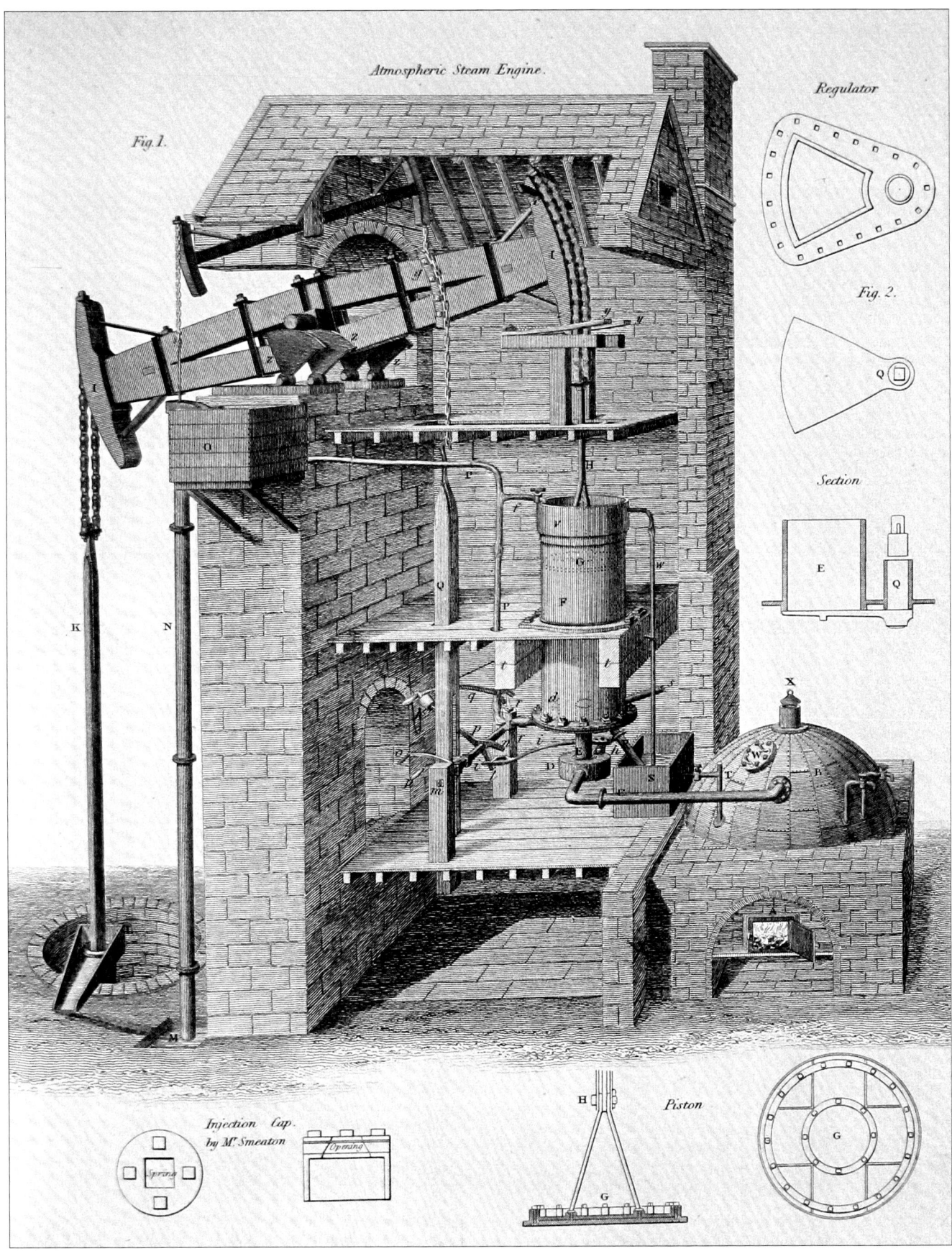

This engraving shows a Newcomen Engine with external boiler attributed to John Smeaton from around 1780. Smeaton was a successful improver of Newcomen engines and is understood to have made a series of experiments to determine ideal engine dimensions and arrangements.

Reproduced by courtesy Ironbridge Gorge Museums Trust

THE HISTORICAL, INDUSTRIAL, TECHNICAL AND LOCAL CONTEXT

1.1 Introduction

The development of the Newcomen engine, often referred to as Atmospheric or Fire Engine due to the sources of its power, has been set out in a number of books and articles over the years, many being published by the Newcomen Society itself. My particular interest in the South Gloucestershire Coalfield prompted research into the four engines commissioned at Coalpit Heath between 1751 and 1791. Whilst the main reference sources for these, the Ashton Court papers in the Bristol Records Office and the Middleton Records held at Nottingham University archives are relatively well known, only Ken Rogers has published anything in depth on the subject of Newcomen Engines in the Bristol Region.[1] This account is concerned with an analysis of the bills relating to the first of these engines to be commissioned in 1751.

1.2 The Bristol and Coalpit Heath Coalfield

The industrial revolution, that confluence of inventive and commercial energy that enabled Great Britain to enjoy global economic pre-eminence depended to a large extent on the conjunction of three factors:

- The country's relative political stability and the consequent growth of the wealth and entrepreneurship of the merchant classes.
- The diversity and accessibility of the country's mineral resources.
- The combination of circumstances that produced an environment that encouraged the commercial application of new discoveries and inventions.

These factors enabled this country to enjoy a long period of commercial and military leadership, the fruits of which we continue to enjoy. At this time Bristol's position as the second largest city was, to a considerable extent, due to its maritime and industrial power base, its easily accessible coal reserves being an important contributor to this.

Although the collieries around Coalpit Heath in the Parish of Westerleigh (now part of South Gloucestershire) were disadvantaged compared to their competitors at Kingswood by their relative distance from the industries of Bristol, they had access to a healthy rural market.

The recorded history of coal mining in the parish goes back to 1301[2] and from 1600 onwards, the available archive materials indicate the scale of the industry. The phases of development of the industry locally can be summarised as follows:

- Pre 1700 – Extensive small scale mines operated by the tenants of the land with shafts up to about 90 feet deep, subject to frequent flooding.
- 1700-1750 – Progressive concentration of the mineral rights and the mines in the hands of the Lords of the Manor of Westerleigh (hereafter abbreviated to LoW) and the development of improved drainage of mines.

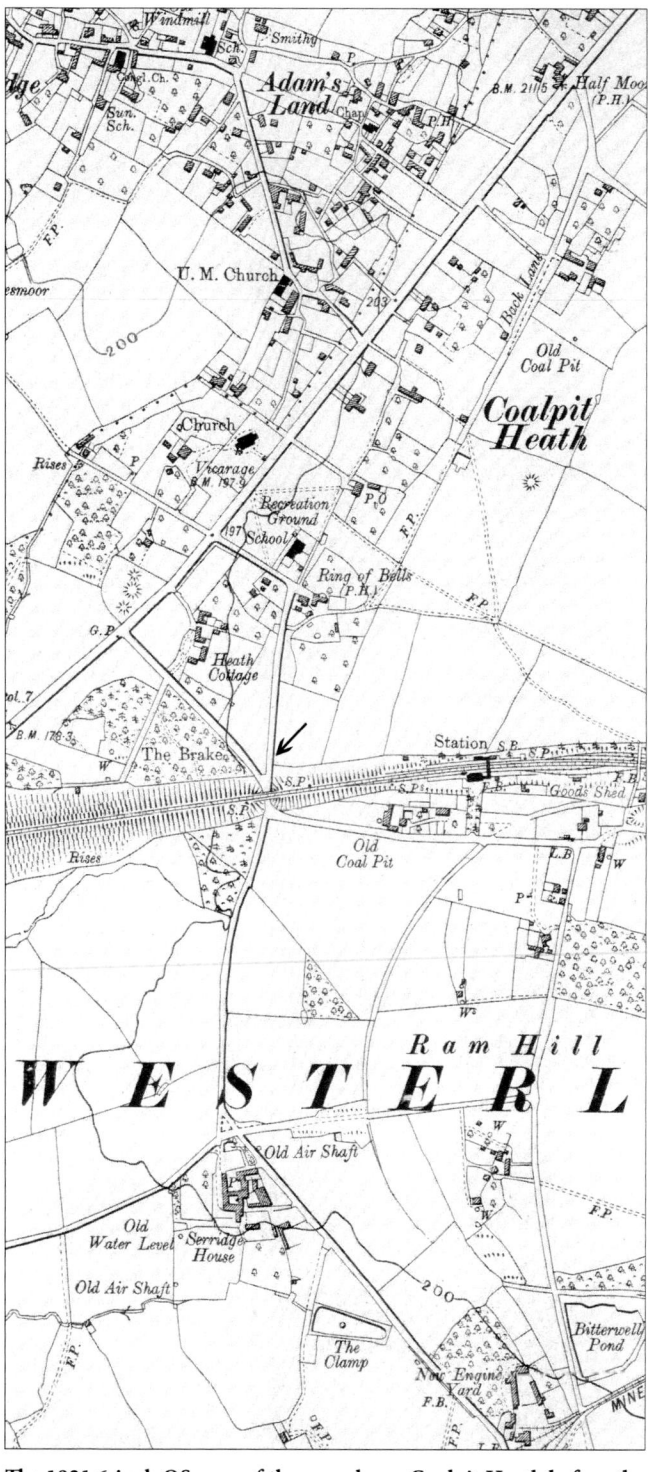

The 1921 6-inch OS map of the area shows Coalpit Heath before the housing developments of the 1970s and 1980s. The ex GWR London to South Wales line (Badminton Extension) cuts across the centre of the area. The Badminton Road (the current A432) cuts diagonally across the area and the section to the east has been worked extensively for coal since medieval times. The variety of mining features in the area being obvious from even a brief examination. The location of the 1751 engine just north of the railway line is indicated by a small arrow.

- 1750-1800 – Introduction of steam pumping power and formalised management methods together with full control of the coalfield by LoW.
- 1800-1860 – Fuller exploitation of all the coal seams as the introduction of railways eases transport problems.
- 1853-1949 – The working life of Frog Lane Colliery the last local mine (all other local pits closed by 1870).[3]

1.3 The Newcomen Engine

Thomas Newcomen's atmospheric engine provided the first reliable source of power that was not wind, water or animal dependent. His first engine is understood to have been installed at Dudley in the Black Country in 1712 (there is a strong case for this being preceded by at least one Engine in Cornwall). Whilst the subsequent take up of this technology was rapid by the standards of the day, it was impaired by high cost (which until the 1730s also included royalties) and the uncertainty of its payback. By 1751 around 250 Newcomen engines are understood to have been installed nationally.[4]

At this point it may be helpful to revisit the basic functions of the Newcomen engine and as Dr Raistrick's description cannot be improved on it is included here[5]. Inserted in brackets are the letters that cross reference the main components with the simple diagram below:

'In this engine, Newcomen used a vertical cylinder (P), closed at the bottom end, with a moveable piston which could travel the length of it. The piston was suspended from the end of a beam which was pivoted near the middle (E) like a giant see-saw. The cylinder was connected to a boiler (A) so that steam could be admitted to the cylinder below

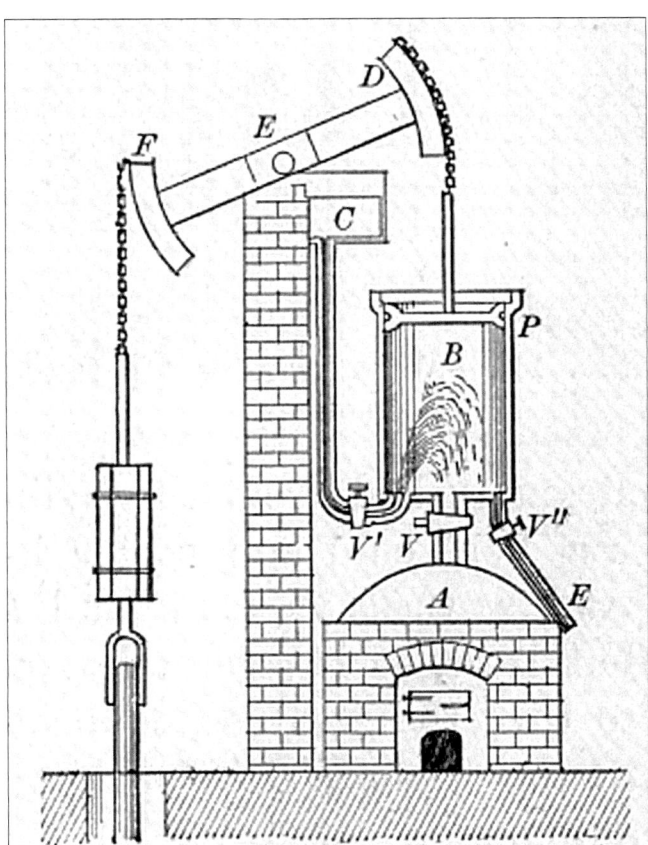

the piston (B), which by the weight of the pump rods hung from the other end of the beam (F) , and helped slightly by the steam was drawn to the top of its stroke.

When the cylinder had filled with steam, the steam valve (V) was closed and a jet of cold water injected (V1), which caused the condensation of the steam and the production of a partial vacuum, so that the weight of the atmosphere on top of the piston forced it down, and so, through the beam, raised the pump rods and pump buckets attached to the other end. By this repeated stroke, the pumps were worked with normal action. The steam did not need to have a pressure greater than that of the atmosphere, so that the boilers did not need to be very strong and in fact were at the beginning made of copper, and sometimes with a leaden top.'

Dr Raistrick also described the process of sourcing and assembling the components and this is also included here to set the scene for my subsequent interpretation of the bills:

'The steam engines that were being erected by Newcomen and others under this patent, employed in their erection many different craftsmen, and parts were supplied from different sources. The engine was not yet in any sense a unit, built to a basal uniting frame or base plate, and sent out by a particular maker, but consisting of a number of parts which were incorporated with the boiler into a special building. The whole structure – boiler, engine parts, pipework and building were assembled together by carpenter, mason, plumber, blacksmith and engineer, the various materials being bought piecemeal from the most convenient or best suppliers. An order was thus given, not for an engine but for a cylinder and cylinder bottom; pipes might be got from the same maker or another; rods and wrought iron work came from the forge or blacksmith, and some parts, like the piston, might need wrought and cast iron in combination.

Among the principal parts of the engine the largest casting is of course the cylinder, the cylinder bottom to which most of the pipework connects is a separate casting. The piston head (described as "piston plate") was also cast. The pipe work was very varied – a short large diameter pipe for the steam connection between boiler and cylinder; the eduction pipe for exhaust water and air; the injection pipe for the water spray which condenses the steam, and numerous smaller pipes connected with the water supply and cistern. Bars and sleepers of cast iron are used for the furnace grate and for some of the structural supports. The main weight of the cylinder is carried by cross beams of timber and the main beam of the engine, until a later date, was also built up of timber, these being the main part of the carpenters work. There was a good deal of blacksmiths and engineers work in the strapping of the beam and the structure of the arch heads at the beam ends. The bearings and the many rods and levers which worked the various valves of the engine would also have been made from scratch by the smiths.'

So each engine installation was a bespoke project, built to the designs of the engine wright and based on his knowledge of what had worked previously.

These days we are so familiar with and dependent on the outputs of global mass production that it is easy to forget that this is relatively recent phenomena, as recently as a hundred years ago many everyday products could still be described as being hand made. This may lead us to discount the achievements of the early engineers and engine wrights who had to design, manufacture and assemble every component of the early Newcomen Engines and then adjust them to ensure they worked effectively.

1.4 The Coalpit Heath Colliery Owners

The Lords of Westerleigh (LoW), Messrs Smith, Middleton and Colston, were an industrial partnership formalised in 1746 with the apparent intention of developing the mineral resources of the area. Jarrit Smith, who had strong local connections, holding half the shares and the others a quarter each.[6] These shares in the Manor of Westerleigh had come down via relationships by marriage to the three daughters of Samuel Astry, originally Lord of the Manor of Westerleigh from 1667 to 1704. It was Astry who first started to systematically exploit the local Coal measures, apparently commissioning the construction of the 'great levelle' to lower the local water table around 1700.

The mouth of the drainage level on the River Frome at Damsons Bridge, thought to have been built by Samuel Astry c.1700. It provided an outlet for the water raised by the 1791 Serridge Engine and may also have connected with the 1751 and the other two engines. Its full extent is uncertain and research on its route continues.

It appears that one of the early initiatives of the new partnership was to develop their deeper coal measures and in 1749 this led to the decision to invest in a Newcomen engine to dewater the seams at the southern end of the Coalpit Heath coalfield. It is likely that Smith and Colston would have been aware of earlier successful installations of similar engines in Bristol and elsewhere.

It is also known that Lord Middleton, an experienced Nottinghamshire coal mining operator, had prior experience of such engines at Wollaton as early as 1728[8] and subsequently at his Trowell Field collieries in 1733[9], both in Nottinghamshire.

The 1751 Coalpit Heath engine was not however the first to be commissioned locally, the LoW were just beaten to it by Charles Bragge and his partners who in 1750, purchased components for an Engine for their Nibley Coal Works, a mile or so north and at the opposite end of the local coal basin (the cylinder was 36-inch diameter and had been ordered by the Warmley Brass company from Coalbrookdale but returned in favour of a larger one[10]). It is pure conjecture on the author's behalf but was Jarrit Smith influenced in his decision to install a Newcomen engine by hearing of, and later seeing, the preparation work going on at Nibley, which would have just been visible to him from the top floor of his residence at Mayshill Farm.

As early as 1719, the purchase of a Newcomen Engine had been seriously considered by Sir Alexander Cuming who was working the coal on his Serridge estate, a few hundred yards south of where the 1751 engine was built, but no evidence has been found to confirm that this progressed beyond the planning stage.[11]

1.5 What the 1751 Engine House Looked Like

Although there are examples of Newcomen Engine Houses remaining both locally and across the rest of the UK, styles vary considerably and for many of those that have been demolished, no photographic or other images are available. However, in this case, it is fortunate that the Bristol Records Office holds two copies of the 1772 Maps of the Parish of Westerleigh drawn up by Hall[12], which show clear representations of the four Coalpit Heath Engine Houses. These maps were delineated in the contemporary pictorial style by Sturge in 1786, fourteen years after Hall's survey, and whilst the representations of the engine houses differ between the two copies of the maps (apparently being drawn by different artists) their main features are identical. The rationale for determining the building dates for each engine and the background to the maps is set out in section 4.3.

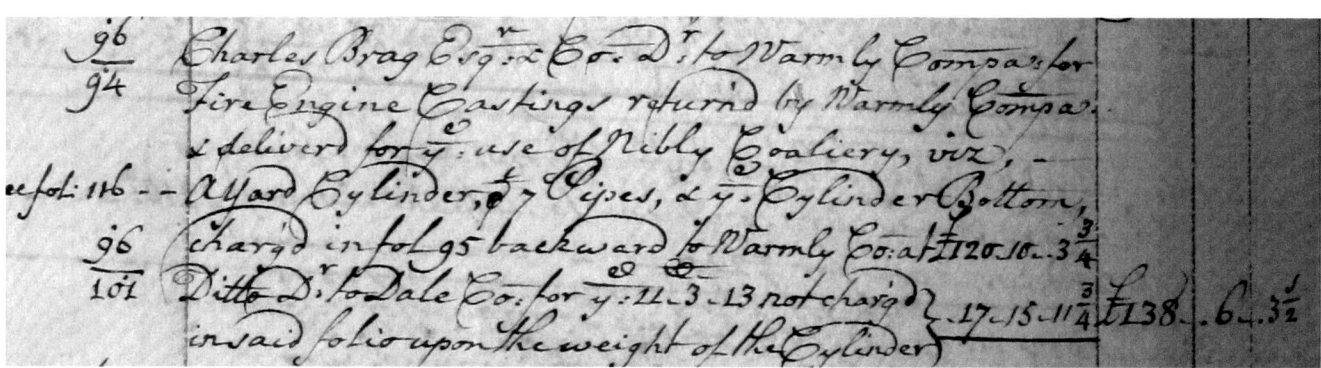

This 1750 entry from Goldney's Account Book gives descriptions and costs of the cylinder and other parts supplied by Coalbrookdale for the first engine at Nibley operated by Bragge and Partners. *Reproduced by courtesy of the WRO*

Hall's map of the Parish of Westerleigh was drawn up in 1772. Two copies are held in the Bristol Records Office under reference AC/PL 89-1 and 2. The left-hand image is an enlargement from the former of the engine understood to have been the 1751 engine, that on the right is from the second copy of Halls 1772 Map (AC/PL/89-2) and shows the same engine house but appears to have been drawn in a different hand.

Both reproduced by courtesy of the BRO

The main features of note from the illustration of the engine believed to be the 1751 one are as follows:

A. The Engine house appears to be round (i.e. with a circular plan) a most unusual feature.

B. The boiler, the round topped feature on the left hand side, appears to be outside the Engine House. It has been generally understood that until the late 18th century, boilers were contained within the engine house. External boilers did not often warrant a dedicated house. This topic is examined in more detail in Chapter 4.

C. The balance beam with its semi-circular arch head emerges from the top right-hand side of the engine house with the pump rods suspended from it and the head frame around them.

D. What appears to be scaffolding on the left of the engine house is probably the chimney.

E. The map shows three windows on the engine house, suggesting that it had three separate storeys above ground level.

F. The purpose of the low square feature to the far right of the house is unclear, it may be the 'balance box' linked by levers to the pitwork to counterbalance their weight.

1.6 The archive sources

The primary archive sources on which this account is based are the Ashton Court papers, held under reference AC/AS xxx in the Bristol Records Office (hereafter abbreviated to BRO) and the Middleton papers (held under reference Mi Av xx) in the University of Nottingham archives (hereafter abbreviated to Notts Univ.) The central material for this account are the fifteen suppliers bills for the engine's construction, individual references for which are given in section 1.8 and full transcriptions in Chapter 3. Both archives hold additional estate records, summary accounts and notes of payments made to these suppliers, which are not described in detail in this account.

Thomas Goldney's original bill for the castings from Coalbrookdale is also held by the Wiltshire & Swindon History Centre in the account book maintained by Goldney between 1744 and 1769. It was Roger's discovery of this that resulted in his 1972 book *The Newcomen Engine in the West of England*. With this notable exception, the author is not aware of further analysis of this source or indeed of any organised study of Newcomen Engines specific to the Bristol region.

Some of the BRO materials have been referred to by Rogers and some are duplicated in both Record Offices. In 2008, following a thorough review of the Middleton Papers, a further series of previously unreported bills were identified, providing additional detail, including most usefully, two more of Charles Palmers bills. Palmer appears to have had overall responsibility for the commissioning of the engine and presented three separate bills covering labour, materials and sundries respectively. All three provide useful insights, highlighting the patterns of on site activity, the variety and sources of the materials and Palmer's role in paying for drinks and tips for workmen at the major construction milestones.

The Palmers appear to have been a Mangotsfield based family of engine wrights, records of their involvement in this business can be found from 1744 to 1791. An outline of the known references to the Palmer family is set out in Appendix 2.

1.7 The Sequence of the Bills

The earliest bill that refers specifically to work on the Engine is Palmer's labour bill which records that his team are working on site from the 27th October 1750. This is quickly followed by Palmer's materials bill, commencing on the 13th of November. Under what appears to be Palmer's overall direction we then see brasswork being supplied by James Malcott and Nathaniel Arthers' team of smiths starting work, both in early December 1750.

Robert Taylor, who appears to be a local haulier is busy at the same time bringing in stone, bricks, timber, mortar and lime described as '*for ye use of ye fire engine*'.

The large castings (the cylinder and base) were supplied by the Coalbrookdale company through Goldney's agency, the first bill being dated 21st January 1751. This and other entries are adjusted to the Gregorian calendar, the transition to which was made in this very year. Goldney's large castings are followed three days later by Thomas Hill's lead top for 'the boyler'. Bills from these and other suppliers continue until April 1751.

It is believed the engine started work in early May 1751. This deduction is made on the basis that all materials appear to have been supplied and most work completed by April and only Palmer and members of his team remain on site, charging for working round the clock for two weeks from 20th April (Palmer's first bill). At this point the total bills amount to £877 16s 1¼d.

After almost a year's interval in April 1752, during which only Palmer bills occasionally, a further series of bills indicate additional work being required on the engine and these continue intermittently for a further four years. In this case, Nathaniel Arthers' blacksmiths appears to be using materials supplied by Hillhouse Getley. These bills appear to duplicate a number of items previously supplied, suggesting that some of the original items needed to be replaced. These bills amount to £115 3s 8¼d, much less than the original total but a significant amount nonetheless. No charges from Palmer for this period have surfaced; suggesting either that he was not employed because of dissatisfaction with his initial work or simply because he was busy elsewhere. Palmer and his descendents did work for LoW on subsequent Newcomen installations (See Appendix 2).

1.8 SUMMARY OF BILLS FOR THE 1751 COALPIT HEATH 'FIRE ENGINE'

Records Office Ref.	Suppliers Name and Business	Summary of Material and Services Supplied	First date	Last Date	Totals in £ s d
Nott's Univ' Mi Av 171/4	Charles Palmer 'Engineer'	This bill (the only one not transcribed) is for labour from Palmer and his team	27.10.1750	13.03.1752	114.14. 6
Nott's Univ' Mi Av 168/43	Robert Taylor 'Haulier'	Haulage of heavy loads – this bill is "for the Fire Engine' and ties with Goldney's and Hill's bills	29.10.1750	22.05.1751	42.16. 6
Nott's Univ' Mi Av 168/39	Charles Palmer 'Engineer'	This bill is for materials only (iron and steel in this case) and notes that they are for his and Hillhouses use	5.11.1750	13.07.1751	80. 3. 2½
Nott's Univ' Mi Av 171/5	Charles Palmer 'Engineer'	This is his sundries bill and covers items such as drink, bricks etc and is the most informative	17.11.1750	19.04.1751	27. 4.10
Nott's Univ' Mi Av 168/40	Nathaniel Arthers 'Blacksmith'	Arthers and his blacksmiths are working to prepare Goldney's castings and make other parts	5.12.1750	1.05.1751	90.12.10
Nott's Univ' Mi Av 168/69	James Malcott 'Brass Merchant'	Various items in brass	11.12.1750	6.06.1751	37. 7.10½
Nott's Univ' Mi Av 168/35	John Willets and Geo Wilding 'Iron Merchants'	Boiler Plates were sent from Willets forge at Wednesbury to Wilding at Framilode	9.01.1751	21.02.1751	60. 0. 9
Nott's Univ' Mi Av 168/41	Thomas Goldney 'Coalbrookdale'	Goldney held the agency in Southwest England for castings from the Coalbrookdale Co.	21.01.1751	22.04.1751	307. 3. 0¾
Nott's Univ' Mi Av 168/37	Thomas Hills 'Lead Merchant'	Hills is charging for lead and the services of his men to make it to the required forms	24.01.1751	9.04.1751	88. 0.11½
Nott's Univ' Mi Av 171/8	William Ponsford	Small amounts of leather, presumably for clacks etc	8.04.1751	-	9. 9. 5
Nott's Univ' Mi Av 168/38	W'm Tily 'Timber Merchant'	Elm Planks of differing thicknesses and charges for halling (i.e. haulage)	Paid on 3.02.1752		3. 0. 0
Nott's Univ' Mi Av 194/3	Hillhouse Getley & Co. 'Iron Merchants'	Appears to be for Iron and Brass Work – some dates coincide with Arthers' bill above so is probably for related work	20.04.1752	14.07.1754	64.12. 5
BRO AC/AS 97/3	Nathaniel Arthers 'Blacksmiths'	Arthers and his smiths appear to be working with Hillhouse Getley	19.06.1752	18.11.1754	31.19. 9¼
BRO AC/AS 93/3	Geo Wilding 'Iron Merchant'	Boiler Plates	30.08.1755	8.09.1755	18.11. 6
				TOTAL	£975.19. 9½

11 Nov.r 1751

Bills sent from Westerleigh of the perticular Expences of the
Fire Engine there set up in the year 1750.

£   s   d

To W.m Tily's Bill for Plumplanhre &c .... 3 .. 0 .. 0

To James Malliott for Brasses &c .... 37 .. 7 .. 10½

To George Wilding for Boiler plates &c .... 60 .. 0 .. 0

To Thomas Stibbs for Lead work, Soder &c .... 00 .. 0 .. 11½

To James Millhouse Ironmonger .... 02 .. 5 .. 0½

To Nath: Arthurs for smith work .... 90 .. 12 .. 10

To Tho: Goldney & C.o for the Cylinder Barrells &c 307 .. 3 .. 0½

660 .. 10 .. 5½

To Palmer the Engineers Bill which Mr Smith
has not sent, but beleieves will amount to .... 100 .. 0 .. 0

To money already paid for work at the fire
Engine as by a perticular taken from the
Clark's Books .... 259 .. 9 .. 9

To Palmers an additional Bill on acc.t of the fire
Engine .... 102.0 .. 0 .. 2½
110 .. 19 .. 0

Note there is 31 .. 0 .. 0 paid Palmer in the perticular
which I apprehend is towards his Bill

I don't see any Bill for Timber

To Pitchfords Bill for Leather &c .... 9 .. 9 .. 0

Totale 1138 .. 19 .. 2½

£ 1148 .. 0 .. 2

This account, dated November 11th 1751 appears to be an attempt to establish the full costs of the engine, in addition to summarising the bills it contains an entry to money already paid etc which the author believes is an internal charge from the LoW estate – see 2.6.
Reproduced by courtesy of the University of Nottingham Manuscripts and Special Collections (Ref Mi E 9-13)

1.9 Some Questions

The review of the archive materials raises two questions: Firstly, from the map (the only pictorial evidence), the engine house appears to be round, a most unusual and distinctive feature. Whilst the forms of Newcomen engine houses vary widely, most are square or rectangular with the exception of another round one commissioned by Thomas Goldney in 1764 to pump the water for the fountains in the garden of his house in Bristol.[13] Given Goldney's involvement with supplying materials and the proximity in time and distance, was there a connection here?

There are other instances of round Engine Houses (such as the 19th century Cruquius multi beam engine house in the Netherlands) but these are very much the exception. Halls map shows the 1751 engine house to be circular with a conical roof and whilst initial reactions may be to attribute this to the map maker's perspective, closer examination confirms that it is deliberate when compared to its nearest neighbour on the same map, only 250 yards distant which is clearly of the more typical rectangular form.

This round form is confirmed in a document concerning the 1791 Serridge Engine (500 yards distant), written by Messrs James (Bailiff) and Humphreys (Clerk) in 1792 referring to surplus engine parts being stored in the old round engine house, suggesting that this engine was not in use by then.[14]

Secondly why was another Newcomen Engine commissioned c1765 within 250 yds distance? By contrast archive material for this machine is notable by its absence and it is only Hall's maps and one other that confirm its existence.[15]

There is no obvious answer for this, but the author believes that the major failure which occurred around Christmas 1753 and the apparent early demise of the 1751 engine, both of which are examined in more detail later, may have been factors in this.

The rectangular engine house that is understood to have been built around 1765 located 250 yards west of the 1751 engine as shown on the first version of Hall's map, BRO AC/PL 89-1.

Reproduced by Courtesy of the BRO

CHAPTER 1 References

1. K. Rogers, *The Newcomen Engine in the West of England* (Moonraker Press 1976) ISBN 239001575.
2. Frampton Cotterell Local History Society, *Images of England – Frampton Cotterell and Coalpit Heath* (Tempus 2007), ISBN 9780752444116, p7.
3. SGMRG & Y&DHC, *Frog Lane Colliery 60 Years On* (Lightmoor Press 2009) ISBN 9781899889334.
4. J. Kanefsky and J. Robey, Steam Engines in 18th Century Britain: A Quantitative Assessment Technology and Culture, vol 21 no 2 (April 1980), pp161-186.
5. A. Raistrick, *Dynasty of Ironfounders* (Ironbridge Gorge Museums Trust, reprinted 1989), ISBN 185072 0584, pp127-8.
6. Nottingham University Archives (NU), Middleton Collection Uni MiDA SS1/7 ND. This clearly sets out the dates and sequence of the changes in the Middleton holdings in the Manor of Westerleigh.
7. The earliest reference to Newcomen Engine installations in the Bristol area is contained in the 1741 minutes of the Court of Directors of the Chelsea Waterworks held in the London Metropolitan Archive (LMA) under reference ACC255-CH-01 010. These establish that John Wise, an engine wright from Hawkesbury, Warwickshire (where there was a concentration of early Newcomen Engines) built three engines at Brislington, Hanham and Kingswood between 1737 and 1741. It is possible that Wise built further engines in the Bristol area.
8. L. T. C. Rolt & J. S. Allen, *The Steam Engine of Thomas Newcomen* (Landmark Publishing 1997). ISBN 190152244, p151.
9. *Ibid* p154.
10. K. Rogers, Ref 1, p30.
11. GA 421/E64 *Nota I have Agreed wth ye proprietors of ye Fire Engine Company for Liberty to set Up a Fire Engine upon any part of my Estate paying them Yearly £35 wch is £100 less than* [ever] *they gave a licence for any other wch they Agreed to to prevent ye Reversing of their Patent wch was really no new Invention of Savorys but discovered by the Marquis of Worcester in a Book dedicated to King & Parliament many years Ago And Severall Members of Parliamt having at my desire agreed to Contribute a Sume of Money for voiding ye Grant in order to wch there was a Bill to have been brought in by ye advise of ye* [Govt] *attorney Gen^{ll} Sr Edwr^d Northy.*
12. BRO AC/PL/89/1 and 2.
13. K. Rogers, ref.1, p35.
14. BRO AC/AS 97-12.
15. BRO 31965[STG]/94 and Coal Authority Map Ref. R333.

This is the other round Newcomen engine house locally, commissioned by Thomas Goldney in 1764 to pump water for the fountain in the grounds of his house in Clifton. It had (latterly) a cylinder of 15in. x 9ft 2in.

The 54-inch Newcomen engine built by Francis Thompson in 1791 for Oakerthorpe Colliery in Derbyshire. Pictured here c.1915 at the Pentrich Colliery near Chesterfield to where it was moved in 1841. It worked until around 1918 and was then acquired by the Science Museum in 1920, dismantled and rebuilt in their main entrance hall.

Reproduced by courtesy of the Science Museum/Science & Society Picture Library

Chapter 2
BUILDING THE ENGINE, HOUSE and PITWORK

2.1 Introduction

This chapter concentrates on describing the sequence of construction and the interactions between the various suppliers and their work. Supporting information on proportions, weights, dimensions etc for a Newcomen Engine of this size are included to provide a fuller picture. Much of this information is drawn from the work of John Curr 'Superintendent of the Coal Works' for the Duke of Norfolk's Sheffield collieries in 1797 who published a guide setting out the recommended dimensions and proportions of all parts of Newcomen engines, their houses and pumping arrangements.[1]

It was the detail and interrelated nature of the suppliers' bills that prompted production of this account. Whilst it is believed that all bills for the mechanical items have been located, those for the basic construction materials are absent and are thought to have been provided by the LoW estate. With some contextual data and interpretation, it is possible to identify what these were and when they were supplied.

2.2. The Investment Case c.1749

In 1749 as today, entrepreneurs sought opportunities to invest in their operations to generate greater income. Having worked the coalfield for a little time the LoW could be expected to be familiar with the local geology and potential of the coal underneath their and other local estates. Although Astry is understood to have constructed his 'great levelle' around 1700 (see Section 1.4) to lower the height of the water table and enable the coal seams to be worked, the majority of the coal was at still greater depth.

The total cost of commissioning the Fire Engine at £975 19s 9d was a vast amount in those days that could only be recouped by increased coal sales and the LoW would have recognised the revenues available from the newly accessible coal. As their partnership was still in its early stages and this was probably their first major joint investment, it could be speculated as to whether this idea was in Jarrit Smith's mind when he instigated the arrangement. He would have been familiar with the local geology and the potential of Newcomens invention had been widely publicised.

Although the technology of the atmospheric engine was well established by this time, such an investment was still risky as failures of Newcomen installations were frequent and the geology of coal seams is never certain until worked.

2.3 Selecting the Site for the Pumping Shaft C1749

Pumping shafts, as distinct from those used to wind coal (which were wound by horse gins until well into the C19) were typically sunk to the lowest feasible point on the 'dip' of the seams and were normally completed before work on engine building started. Few seams were absolutely flat and if water was pumped from the lowest available part of the 'dip', the effect of gravity makes extraction of the uphill coal easier (known as working 'to the rise'), and of course it would be dry. Before Newcomen's invention, water was removed by winding it up in large buckets or primitive pumps worked by horse gins. Wind and water power were also used where available but we have no evidence for this in Coalpit Heath.

The main considerations for determining where the pumping shaft was to be sunk were (and still are):

- Identifying the lowest reachable point on the dip of the coal seams
- Ensuring the strata would support a shaft (unstable ground and underground water feeders were the main problems at this time)
- Making sure that the water pumped out did not go straight back underground.

The 1751 Engine was built on the south western edge of the Coalpit Heath Coal basin from where the coal seams dip generally to the east. There are three workable seams of coal here, the Hard Vein being uppermost, the Hollybush next and the High Vein underneath. There are no records of the exact shaft depth but if sunk to the High Vein, it would be around 190 feet deep.

Neither is the diameter of the pumping shaft known but the top of the Ram Engine shaft, sunk around 30 years later, remains visible and is of square form with rounded corners and six feet across. The shaft of the 1751 engine was probably similar.

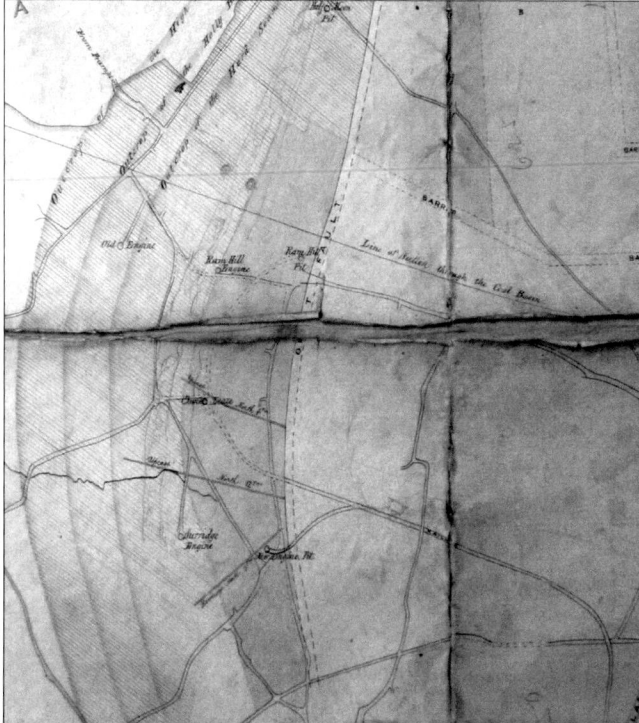

This map is thought to have been drawn up in the 1840s as part of the planning for the sinking of Frog Lane Colliery which began in 1853. It shows quite clearly where the seams outcrop around this western end of the Coalpit Heath Basin. The tear on the map is slightly to the south of and parallel with the later position of the ex GWR London – South Wales railway. The location of the 1751 engine is not marked and is roughly in between Old Engine and Ram Hill Engine.

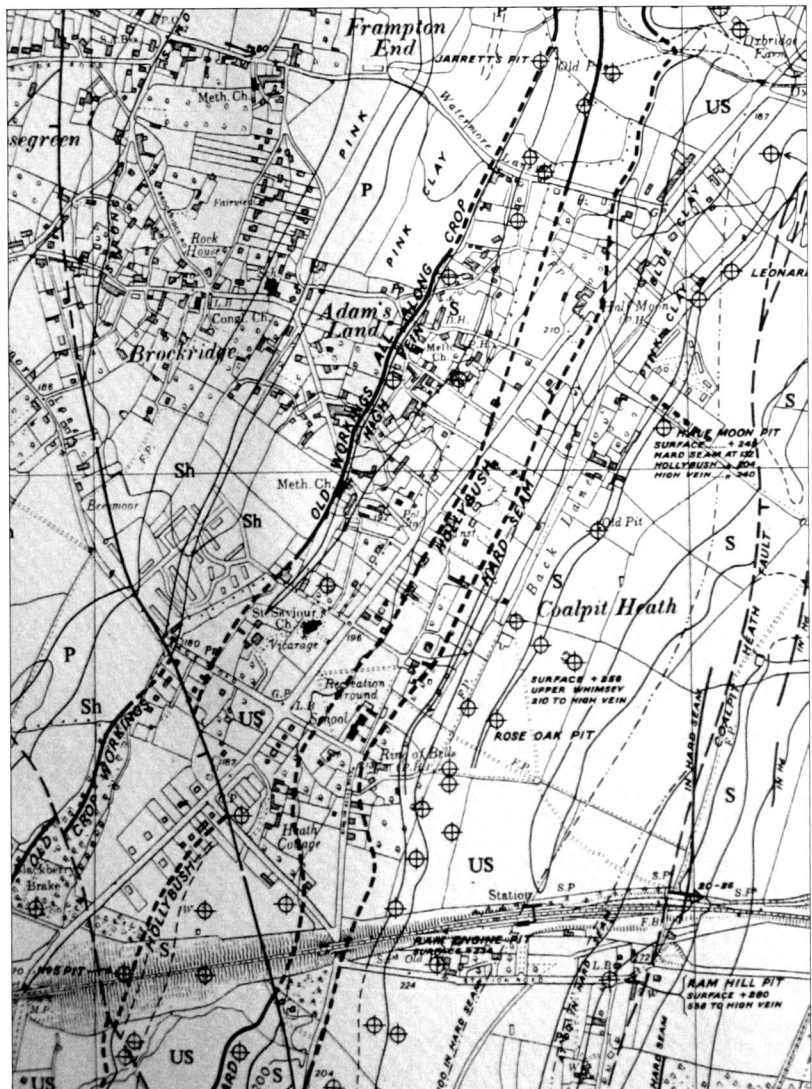

This extract from the geological map show the numbers of shafts sunk locally as well as the position and inclination of the local coal seams. The shaft of the 1751 engine is not marked on the geological map, presumably because it was disused and filled before the initial survey. Its location is immediately north of the railway embankment on the dotted line denoting the outcrop of the hard seam. The position of the second engine, constructed c1765 is the shaft immediately to the east of that marked 'No 5 pit' underneath the railway embankment. Ram Engine constructed c1784 is shown south of the railway and opposite Coalpit Heath Station.

2.4. Sinking the Shaft c.1749/1750

Shaft sinking was normally undertaken by dedicated teams of experienced miners (known, not surprisingly as 'Sinkers') who charged for their work by the feet or yards depth. They used simple tools such as pick, shovel and crowbar, gunpowder being used where hardness of the rock required. Water was wound out in buckets using a horse gin. Shaft collars (the area immediately surrounding the shaft at surface) were normally reinforced with stonework to ensure stability and shafts would be lined with stone, timber or brick where the strata was unstable. There would normally be some form of a sump at the bottom of the shaft to collect water and pump from.

Given the number of pits in the area, shaft sinking would have been a routine activity locally, with the teams of sinkers moving to the next site as soon as their work on one shaft was complete. The LoW would probably have used their own team of sinkers rather than bringing in teams from elsewhere.[2] This may explain why no separate bills for shaft sinking have been identified as these costs would have been part of the estate's normal mining work.

The best way of removing water raised from underground is to divert it into an available drainage adit or level (a gently sloping tunnel ending at the lowest accessible point on a nearby stream or river) Such arrangements had two

advantages, firstly saving the work of pumping the water the additional height to the surface and secondly reducing the likelihood of the water returning directly underground. The arrangement for routing the water from the shaft into the adit needed to ensure that the flow did not reverse. This was addressed by constructing a launder (a one way gate) and lodge (a reservoir) as part of shaft sinking and lining. If an adit was not available the water would be raised to the surface and routed into the nearest stream or river.

As far as we know Astry's 'great levelle' of 1700 was very close and would be an ideal destination for the water and this is likely to have influenced the site chosen for the shaft. No maps exist of the route of this level but it is generally understood to run just to the west of and parallel to the Badminton Road, less than 200 yards from the engine site. It is reasonable to assume that a short branch to connect the pumping shaft to the level was built.[3]

2.5. Planning the Engine – Autumn 1750

Once the shaft was sunk the depth that the water was to be pumped from and its volumes would be known. This would enable detailed planning for the engine and house to begin as the pumping capacity could be determined and arrangements for pit work confirmed (i.e. size of pump rods, number of lifts, locations of the launders and lodges, shaft fittings etc)

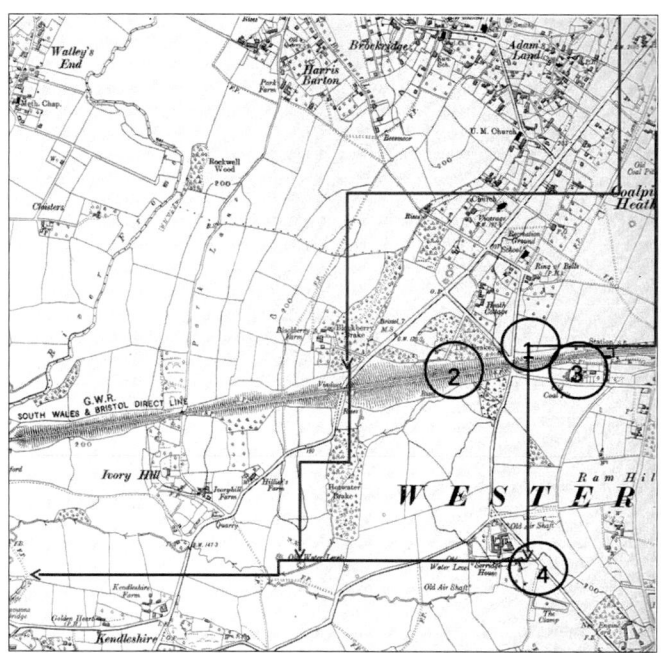

The routes of the Coalpit Heath drainage levels are uncertain and this map shows the conjectural route based on local anecdote. The locations of the 1751 and the three subsequent engines are indicated by numbers showing the sequence in which they were built. It is likely that they were all connected to the level to facilitate removal of the water they raised.

Before sinking the shaft the LoW probably discussed with their agents, bailiffs and overseers the potential of the coal seams and agreed outline plans for their development. When it came to designing and building the engine, Middleton's experience of previous installations in his Nottinghamshire pits would have undoubtedly helped and the LoW would undoubtedly also have consulted widely on the choice of engine wright (in effect a commissioning engineer). Whilst nationally there would have been others capable of such work, it is understandable that they opted for a Charles Palmer as a local man. The LoW came to some form of agreement with Palmer and this is referred to in his bills and their payments to him.

Palmer was probably consulted on engine size and choice of sub contractors and suppliers, presumably favouring those with whom he had worked in the past. The market for the main components i.e. cylinder, pump barrels and related items was dominated at this time by the Coalbrookdale Company on the basis of their casting and boring capabilities (see Chapter 3).

So a 42-inch cylinder, cylinder base and other components that could not be locally manufactured would have been ordered via Goldney from Coalbrookdale, presumably after some preliminary discussions. Details of lead times are unknown but given the circumstances of the period, this would be likely to be months rather than weeks. Work on building the engine house would probably have started around the same time as the order for the cylinder was placed.

A view down the Pentrich pumping shaft clearly showing the three sets of pump rods, the mouth of the rising main and the launder via which water raised was removed from the shaft, the arrangements for the 1751 Engine are likely to have been similar.

Reproduced by courtesy of the Science Museum/Science & Society Picture Library

2.6. Start to Build the Engine House and Related Foundations – October and November 1750

Whilst the construction of the engine house may have been within the capability of the masons employed on the LoW estate it is likely, from the numbers of men employed, that all the building work was undertaken by Palmer's team. The completion of the shaft by the sinkers would have established a clear reference point for location of bob wall, beam and cylinder.

As might be expected, the earliest bills are for Palmer's workmen who started on site on 27th October 1750, followed two days later by Robert Taylor's bills for a days work 'halling lime' with entries for timber and sand a few days later, exactly what you would expect in the early stages of building an Engine House. As Taylor's bills contain numerous entries for 'halling stone' immediately afterwards the presumption is that this was sourced from the LoW quarries. No bills for the supply of this basic building materials have been located so it is likely they were supplied by the LoW estate. It is therefore reasonable to assume that work on the foundations of the Engine House was underway at the start of November 1750. There is an entry on one of the final summary accounts for money *already paid* of £259 which is understood to include at least part of the estate sourced materials for engine house building work.

By the end of November Taylor and his '*plow*' (team of horses) had spent six days hauling timber, thirteen days hauling stones, three days hauling brick, and one each for sand and lime.

Taylor's work continued at a similar rate through December and January and therefore this would seem to be the period when the engine house walls were built, how they protected the slow setting lime mortar from frost damage is unknown. Curr's standard bob wall thickness for a 42-inch engine is given as 44-inches[4] and this alone would require a substantial quantity of

If the quality of the masonry seen in one of the arches of the 1791 Serridge Engine House is any guide, it is expected that the 1751 engine was built to the same high standard from the local pennant sandstone.

material. As this wall carried the beam its stability and strength was crucial to the successful working of the engine.

By the end of November Palmer and five of his men were working a six day week and continued at this rate until the end of March 1751. There are no separate entries for carpentry or masonry and therefore it is presumed that Palmer's men did this work themselves.

There is an intriguing entry in Palmer's sundries bill on 27th November for two lots of timber from Messrs Evans: '*Six large 28 foot [offers] and three round white spars*'. It is suspected that the former are the seasoned timbers that were held together by strapping and suchlike to make up the beam (28 feet is around the right length) whilst the spars are likely to have been the long timbers for the headgear legs, its main purpose being to raise and lower pitwork in the shaft, the length being needed to ensure the sections of pitwork raised would clear the shaft mouth.

2.7 The Blacksmiths Arrive – December 1750

Palmer's materials bill commences on 13th November with entries for iron, steel, anvils and a vice, obvious requirements when setting up blacksmithing operations on site. An entry in his sundries bill for two pairs of smiths bellows the following week confirming this. This correlates with Nathaniel Arthers's bill, for smiths work and related tools on 5th December. The implication is that Palmer and his men get the site smithy ready for the arrival of Arthers' team in early December. The smiths contribution was hugely important as they produced the wide range of ferrous items not supplied by Coalbrookdale such as fire grates, bolts, braces and straps for the beam and all other controls and linkages.

Construction of large machinery in iron was still a relatively new field and when the few remaining engine components of this period are examined, it's clear that the established principles of building machinery in wood are being applied. Tolerances were still large with linkages between components designed to enable regular adjustment. The smith's work of the period was thus concerned with making individual components that were fitted together on a bespoke basis, indeed the whole engine would have been built on this principle.

2.8 Building and Installing the Balance Beam – January 1751

The balance beam is the massive timber baulk, set on the 'bob' wall (especially thick for this purpose), its outdoor end protruding through an arch in the upper part of the engine house, connecting to the pump rods and the indoor end to the piston rod. The bob wall of the engine house would obviously have to be built up to the requisite height ready for the beam installation. The beam needed to be strong enough to withstand the constant movement and so was of massive construction, often weighing five tons or more. Whilst technologies had advanced sufficiently by the 19th century to enable such beams to be made of iron (either cast in one piece or built up from plates) for most of the 18th century these beams were made of wood held rigid by a series of wrought iron straps and bolts.

The beam would have been carefully built up by Palmer's men using seasoned wood from the LoW estate (probably oak) and/or the 28 feet long [offers] detailed in Palmers sundries bill. Seasoned timber was needed to ensure the beam did not

When the pump rods or sections of the rising main needed removing a powerful and slow lift was required for which the motion of a beam engine was unsuitable. Thus all beam engines had a capstan nearby for this purpose, the majority of which were manually powered. Too mundane to attract the attention of most photographers, we are fortunate that Mr Anderson who took the Pentrich images turned his attention to it – the small roof is probably to protect the machinery rather than the men! The route of the rope from the capstan to the small wheel at the top of the sheerlegs via a carefully arranged channel in one of the legs is a fascinating detail. It may be that the 'three round white spars' in Palmer's Sundries Bill were the sheerlegs.

Reproduced by courtesy of the Science Museum/Science & Society Picture Library

warp once in situ. The piston was kept in alignment with the cylinder (as were the pump rods) by making the beam ends bow shaped, and the arrangement was generally known as arch heads. Ironwork for the bolts, strapping and other fixings needed to secure and retain the beam and arch heads would have been made on site by Arthers' men.

Along with the piston and crosshead, effective and robust arrangement and engineering of the arch head and chains was critical to the success of Newcomen engines, as these were the two major points through which the engines power was transmitted. Until the widespread adaption of parallel motion this crude but effective arrangement was the means by which both piston rod and pitwork were kept at right angles to cylinder and pumprods respectively. This view of the arch head, chains and pump rods of the Pentrich engine clearly illustrates the external arrangements.

Reproduced by courtesy of the Science Museum/Science & Society Picture Library

The length of the beam and arrangement of the arch heads needed careful planning and execution so that the chains at each beam end remain at right angles to the cylinder and intended position of the pump rods in the shaft respectively. Arch heads avoided the need for a bearing and were a simple and robust precursor to the later combination of bearings and parallel motion. The beam may have been installed on its bob wall before the cylinder was positioned but it is not known how the beam was raised (see opposite).

The only other bill that can be attributed to construction of the beam is Arthers' charge of just over £2 for one *balance beam gudgeon* on the 16th of January, this costly item will almost certainly be the massive iron mounting block and bearings for the beam, mounted on top of the bob wall.

Left: The arch heads on the smaller and earlier Newcomen Engine thought to have originated at Griff Colliery in the 1720 and now located at Dartmouth. Whilst the construction is simpler and lighter than the later larger engines, the principles are identical.
Image courtesy of Dartmouth Museum

Given that it was moving continually and bore all the power and weight of the engine and pitwork, it is understandable that beams needed to be both heavy and strong. Most early beams would appear to have been made from well seasoned oak, braced and reinforced by wrought iron straps to ensure that the disruption of replacement would never be needed. This image from *Engineering* in 1895 shows the outdoor end of the 66-inch South Liberty Engine that worked from c1765 to 1900. It was offered to the Victoria and Albert Museum by Mr Bush one of the Ashton Vale Coal & Iron company's Directors and the main reason this offer was not accepted was that accommodating the beam at the V&A would have required a major rebuild on account of its weight of over nine tons.

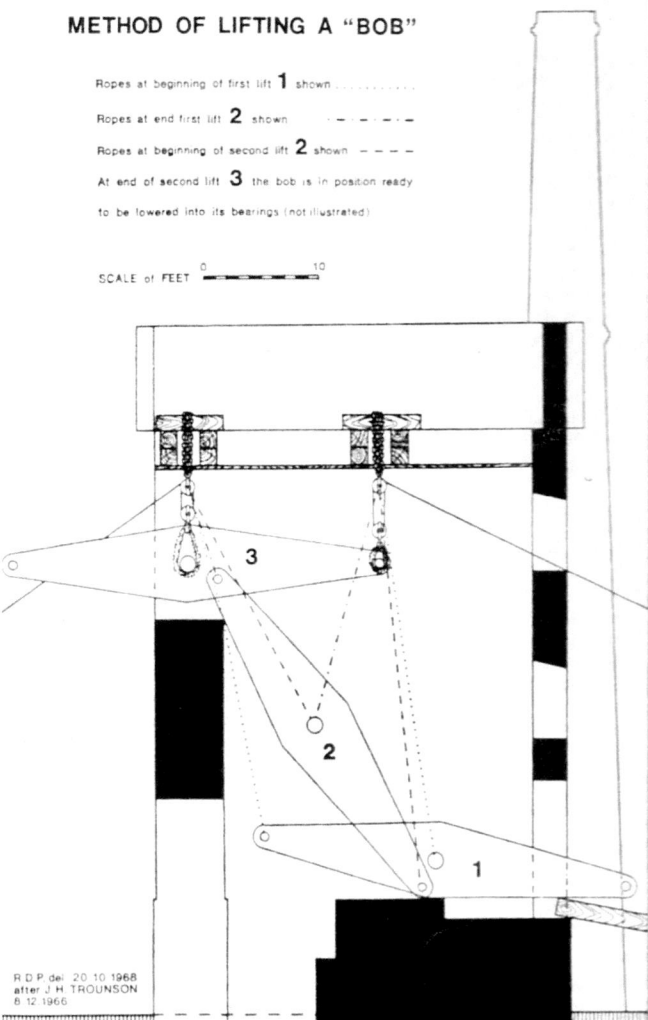

METHOD OF LIFTING A "BOB"

Ropes at beginning of first lift **1** shown . . . .

Ropes at end first lift **2** shown . . — . — . —

Ropes at beginning of second lift **2** shown — — — —

At end of second lift **3** the bob is in position ready

to be lowered into its bearings (not illustrated)

SCALE of FEET

R D P del 20.10.1968
after J H TROUNSON
8.12.1966

This diagram shows how the beams of Cornish engines were raised into position in the 19th century, the main alternative was to build an incline up to the required position and winch the beam up. It is not known which of these was used (if either) for the 1751 engine.

Reproduced by courtesy Trevethick Society

2.9 Install the Cylinder and Base – January 1751

The engine house appears to have been built to the point where it was ready for the cylinder early in January 1751. Palmer's sundries bill shows an entry on the 22nd January *'Paid to the trowmen'* (the men who operated the commercial transport boats up and down the Severn, the major trade artery for much of western England and Wales with direct access to the Coalbrookdale works).

On 24th January, Palmer's bill notes *'Paid Messrs Matthews for loading the cylinder and bottom'*. These items would therefore have arrived from Coalbrookdale by the 22nd, were loaded onto Taylor's Wagon on 24th and taken to site on the 26th January 1751. The difficulty of the task is illustrated by Palmer tipping both the trowmen and the men that loaded and transported the cylinder and bottom. The cylinder (and other heavy items subsequently) were taken only as far as Lawfords Gate (the lower part of Stapleton Rd where the Bristol city wall ended). Taylor's team takes over from here, suggesting that contracts for haulage within the city boundaries were controlled by a cartel of suppliers of which Taylor was not part.

The transport of over three tons of cast iron by wagon and horses the eight or so miles to Coalpit Heath over muddy roads in winter would have been a major undertaking as the area was not served by turnpike roads until later in the century. (See the Vivares engraving, pages 24-25.) Transhipment of this valuable and fragile item from (presumably) a horizontal position on Taylor's wagon to a vertical position inside the engine house would have needed some care and expertise too.

Because of the need for the steam inlet, water injection and exhaust condensate drainage pipes to access the base of the cylinder, it was impractical to mount the cylinder and base directly onto solid masonry which would have been structurally more robust. Instead it was normal practice until the second half of the 18th century to mount the cylinder between two pairs of massive wooden baulks around twelve or fourteen inches square, built into the engine house walls. This was not an ideal approach as the cylinder would need continual attention to stop it 'working' in its mounts. Newcomen Engines with external boilers and therefore with the facility to mount the cylinder directly onto masonry, still needed two large baulks of timber on either side of the upper part of the cylinder to ensure its stability. Tolerances in the space between the baulks and their consistent alignment would have required some skilled three dimensional carpenters and masons work. Presumably Palmer's men handled this although there is no explicit reference to it.

2.10 Build up the Piston – January and February 1751

A seven hundredweight piston plate was delivered at the same time as the cylinder and base. This was in effect the piston face, a massive circle of cast iron, just under 42-inches diameter (to fit the cylinder) and probably about six inches deep. When it arrived, Arthers's men set to work on it billing for *'drilling and cutting 4 new holes in the piston for the braces'*, most likely an early form of crosshead and bearings.

On February 19th Arthers' charges *'for a piston stem and 2 brasses and nuts'*. The stem would be the piston rod, a substantial blacksmith forging of six or so inches diameter, that needed to withstand the stresses and strains generated by each stroke of the engine. This would probably be made in the same manner as anchor shanks (shafts) for ships, a routine product in a maritime city such as Bristol. Thus by the end of February the cylinder would have been in place and the piston and stem assembly complete.

Arthers' bills in December and January for *'Chains'* (expensive ones at £2 and £3 respectively) probably being the massive chains made up of wrought iron links that hung from either end of the beam, connecting the piston and pitwork respectively.

2.11 Building the Boiler, the Fire Grate, Ash Hole and Flues – January to March 1751

Curr's figures suggest that an engine with a 42-inch cylinder would need a boiler of around 15ft diameter,[4] the plates for which would weigh around 4 tons. The boiler was built up from iron plates supplied by Hillhouse Getley and a lead top and pipework installed by Thomas Hills. At this time most boilers were thought to have been of the simple haystack form, with a concave base to provide strength and additional heating area. They were little more than large kettles as the atmospheric engine derived its power from condensation of steam rather than its pressure.

The arrangements of the wrought iron chains on the Pentrich engine are clear in this image, the wear rate on the bearings would have been significant and frequent replacements needed. Inevitably, one wonders what it would have sounded like!

Whilst the cylinder and base were being transported to site, work on the boiler appears to be going on concurrently. The first bills from Thomas Hills, the supplier of the 'lead boyler top', appearing on 24th January 1750, only three days after the date of Goldney's bill for the cylinder. Hills was an existing supplier to the LoW and in other unrelated bills is given the title of 'Plumber'.[5]

The bills from George Wilding, a Framilode based Iron Merchant, tell us that the first of the boiler plates arrive on 9th January. There are five further deliveries of these with the last on 21st February. Taylors 'hallage' bills only once refer to haulage of iron during this period (January 9th itself) so it is probable that Wilding's bill includes his own transport arrangements from Bristol Docks to Coalpit Heath. His reference to 'Freight of 2d per parcel to Bristol' apparently confirming this is the charge for transport from his works at Framilode.

Boiler plates were sheets of wrought iron produced by blacksmiths which needed further cutting, bending and riveting together to make the haystack boiler shape. The dome and all pipework would be fabricated on site from sheet lead and Hill's bill includes '11¾ days' work for two men', assumed to be for making the top and installing the basic pipework junctions.

Taylor's 'hallage' bill for February is mostly concerned with bringing in lead, supporting the case for February being the month in which the boiler and pipework were built.

A boiler full of water could weigh upwards of ten tons and as it was mounted above a largish fire grate area with the ash hole underneath, the foundations would need to be soundly constructed of firebrick. Boiler sides were often encased in masonry to provide additional insulation and support. Below the grate would be the ash pit, normally in the form of a large arched passage, built to

It is not known what shape or form the 1751 boiler took but this image of a disused haystack boiler in use at Pentrich gives some idea of the more common form of early boilers. *Reproduced by courtesy of the Science Museum/Science & Society Picture Library*

Being below the surface and containing little material that is worth recovering, ash pits are often the only feature that survive after Beam engine houses are demolished. Given the appetite of Newcomen engines for coal, the removal of the large volumes of ash and clinker generated needed a passage or tunnel of a size to enable workmen to do this frequently. This example is one of two such features on the 1791 Serridge engine site that may have served such a purpose. Arrangements on the 1751 engine are likely to have been similar. There is strong evidence locally of a healthy demand for such ash as an ideal constituent for lime mortar and local anecdote suggests that building age can be determined by whether the mortar contains such ash and clinker.

facilitate removal of ash. Being below ground level, they often survive long after the engine is scrapped and its house is removed.

Palmer bills for 'Sturbridge Clay' on 23rd February and pays for its loading on 5th March. The high proportion of silica in Stourbridge clay and bricks made them fireproof and was ideal for use around fires and boilers where high temperatures were the norm. It is therefore reasonable to assume that the masonry surrounding the boiler and the ash hole and grate would be under construction at this stage (early March).

Even though the masonry used to support the boiler base and the sides often contained a spiral flue, the available heating surface was limited. There would be an obvious hot spot directly over the fire and scale formation from poor and dirty water would often lead to overheating and damage to the plates.

2.12 Detail Work on the Engine House - January to April 1751
Whilst the major components were being installed and connected, other items not on the critical path could be completed. These are likely to have included:

- Making and installing the controls and valve gear for the engine. Malcott's brasswork bills include valves on 13th Feb and a 'regulater' and 'other work' on March 11th, making up over 60% of his bill.

- Hill's charges in late January for 'sheet lead for cistern in dash', presumably the water cistern installed at the top of the engine house to provide a good head for the water injection into the cylinder.
- William Tily's bill for elm planks on the 3rd of February suggests that this is when the floors and roof timbers are being put in the engine house. Palmer also bills for tiles on 23rd February, presumably for the roof, suggesting the engine house would be substantially complete, the boiler built, the beam probably installed and the house therefore ready to be roofed.

Taylor still brings in a few loads of bricks and stones during late February and March and these would probably be for the ancillary buildings. On April 19th Palmer pays for Stourbridge brick so we can guess this is for the final stages of work to finish off items such as the boiler surround, fire grate chimney, flues etc.

2.13. Fit Out the Engine and Test –April 1751
By the end of March 1751 it would appear that work on the Engine and House was mostly complete with the cylinder, controls, boiler, pipework, beam and fittings in place. The completed engine would then need testing to ensure all components moved in the required manner. This would almost certainly be done manually using pulleys and

ropes to allow precise control and avoid damage. They needed to check that the valve gear operated properly and the beam, piston and pitwork functioned as planned. How and when the arrangements for fire and water would have been tested is unclear but it is expected that the boiler would be filled with water and tested for leaks and then the fire lit and leak testing repeated. They would also want to ensure that the fire, flues and chimney 'drew' properly.

2.14 Installing the Pitwork – April 1751

The mechanical arrangements for raising water in the shaft (generally known as 'pitwork') are complex and only basic details are given here. The main principles being as follows:

- Running the length of the shaft and fixed securely to its side are two or three tubes (later known as 'rising main') made up of sections of iron pipes, (referred to as '*barrels*' in the bills) that ends with the windbore in the sump at shaft bottom.
- Suspended from the chains at the end of the beam and passing down inside the rising main are two or three columns of wooden rods, often termed 'shides' or 'spears'. At regular intervals, these rods pass through and are fixed to the centres of round pistons (called buckets in the bills) that fit snugly inside the rising main. These pistons are fitted with one way valves or flaps called 'clacks' because of the noise they made when closing.
- When the beam rises it lifts the rods, the one way valves close, raising a column of water up the rising main, the top, one of which is discharged via a launder(non return conduit) into a lodge (reservoir) or an adit.
- After the upward stroke, the beam descends (known as going outdoors) and the one way valves open, allowing water to pass through into the buckets and the cycle is repeated, typically between eight and twelve times per minute.
- It was important that the '*barrels*' were accurately bored so that the buckets fitted correctly inside them to minimise leakage.
- The clack valves had leather flaps (gaskets in effect) to seal them, which, with their hinges, were subject to considerable wear and tear from the constant flow of water and the debris contained within it. Therefore at regular intervals along their length, 'clack doors' to facilitate their inspection and repair were built into the pit barrels.
- The rising mains and pump rods were normally organised and installed in two or three stages (or lifts) raising water to intermediate storage lodges rather than a single lift. This arrangement facilitates maintenance, isolates breakages, reduces the weight of water imposed on the pump components and generally avoids single points of failure.
- The diameter of the '*barrels*', the depth of the shaft and the volumes of water would together determine the power needed from the engine. As the volumes of mine water vary according to the seasons, a large contingency of engine power was normally factored in.
- Because the pump rods were under water in the rising main, the net weight of the pump rods inside the barrels was minimal because of the buoyancy of the timber. It was the 'dry' rods above water level in the rising main that added

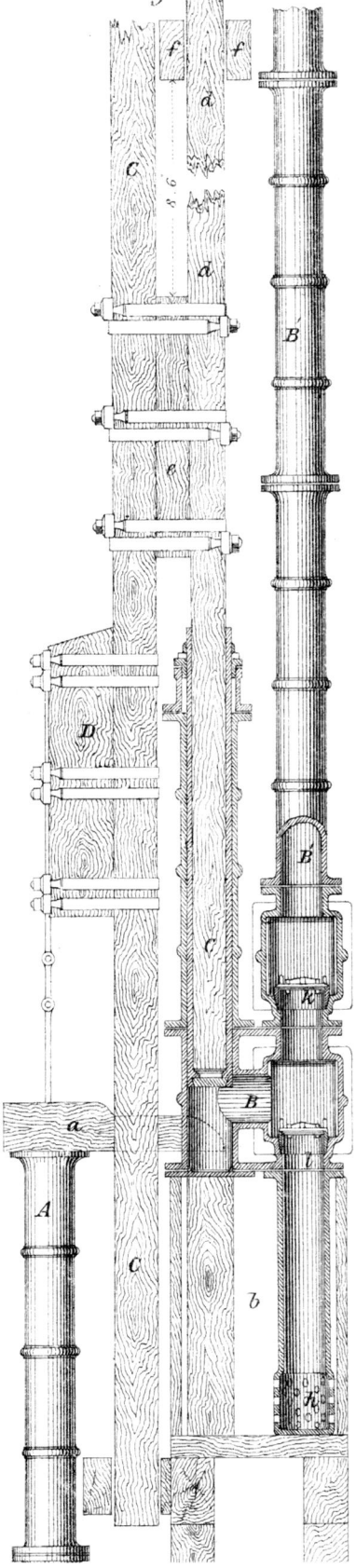

The arrangements shown in this pitwork diagram from the 19th century will not have been very different from those used a century earlier. The vertical motion of the heavily strapped pump rods (C and D) raise water from the rising main pipes (A) that goes via launder (a) to the lodge (b) and is then raised up the next stage in the second raising main(B) via the windbore (h).

22

to the weight of the column of water the beam had to lift. Therefore the length of these dry rods from beam end to barrel top was an important planning consideration.

- There would normally be a series of counterbalance beams and weights linked to the pitwork by levers ensure that the beam was effectively balanced with the bob wall bearing the total weight of all items. There needed to be enough excess weight on the pump rod end of the beam to lower the pitwork and take the engine outdoors.

References in the bills to pitwork include:

- Goldney's bill of April 6th 1751 refers to pit barrels and Palmer's bill of the previous day shows him paying the porters and *'halliers'* for *'loading and hauling pipes'*. Taylor also bills for haulage of pipes on April 16th and May 15th (why the delay?).
- Nathaniel Arthers's bill on February 23rd 1751 for *'iron work for two pairs of buckets and four pairs of flaps'* suggests they are being fitted to the pump barrels at this time.
- Arthers' subsequent bills on April 12th for *chipping the holes in the cast iron* implies that the apertures for clack doors are being cut out of the barrels.
- Goldney's bill of 6th April 1751 for pit barrels, buckets and clacks confirms that the pitwork was being prepared.
- There are bills for *'buckets and flaps'* in this period too from Nathaniel Arthers.
- Palmer's bill for the iron also continues during this period so it is reasonable to assume that this was needed by the smiths to make up for pipework fixings and other shaft fittings.

2.15 Starting the Engine – April and May 1751

There is little data available on commissioning a Newcomen engine but the available sources point to this being a lengthy and somewhat hit and miss process and the experience with commissioning the replica engine at the Black Country Museum in the 1980s would seem to bear this out.

By April 1751 it appears that Palmer's men have the site to themselves and only four of his team are involved, presumably those with most expertise on the engine. In the last week of April he bills nine days for himself and one of his men and seven days for another, indicating that they are working round the clock to get the engine commissioned. Palmer's contract may have required that the engine be ready by a certain date, but the archive materials make no reference to this.

After billing for a full week for himself and one other man in the week of May 4th, the frequency of Palmer's bills reduces significantly, such that by the date of his last bill, ten months later in March 1752, he has only billed 37¼ further days for himself and 62½ days for four others. This is taken to mean that the engine and pitwork are now working and Palmer and selected specialists are attending occasionally to fine tune the engine. Thus it would appear that by the end of May 1751 the LoW had got their new Engine working and were presumably then able to commence laying out the underground workings to extract the coal from the deeper seams.

2.16 The Subsequent Billings

Shortly after Palmer's last bill, a second phase of activity gets under way in April 1752 with Hillhouse Getley billing for raw materials and a range of finished components. This is followed by Nathanial Arthers' bill starting in June 1752 for blacksmiths work. The bills continue for a longer period than the initial series, ending finally in 1756. Despite the fact that neither of these bills refer specifically to either Coalpit Heath or the Fire Engine, there is no doubt in my mind that they are for work on this engine as they refer to work on boiler, regulator, buckets, clacks etc.

The purpose of the work undertaken in this second phase is not immediately clear but correlations between the bills suggests they are undertaking a programme of remedial work to correct defects, both routine and major. These bills are examined in detail in Chapter three and the key points are as follows:

- Major repairs to the pitwork were required in June/July 1752, Hillhouse providing clack seats and some *'boaring'* work on a cylinder.
- In August and October 1753, there are bills for clacks and small cylinders, possibly to repair damage caused by the corrosive action of acidic or sand laden mine water.
- Early in January 1754 it seems there is a more substantial problem; Arthers' bills on January 5th for a new *'regalater'* (albeit substantially cheaper than that originally supplied by Malcott – possibly because it was in iron rather than brass). This is quickly followed by Hillhouse's bill for a *'cylinder board'* weighing 14 cwt. on January 9th. This may have been used to replace the cylinder bottom supplied by Goldney (which was only slightly heavier at 15cwt). The combination of these two breakages would have stopped the engine (i.e. no control and no support for the cylinder), presumably flooding the mine workings.
- Arthers' bills for some new items in the first half of 1754, *'4 sweep bars for ye pistern'* and lots of *'cross headed pins'* (early screws?) and square pins and for *'cutting ye chops'*.
- Both suppliers appear to be working on the boiler in June 1754 as they both bill on 19th June, Arthers' for *hooks and hinges for ye boiler doors* and to *'three men making ye boiler bottom'* whilst Hillhouse bills for a *'door frame'*, thought to be the door for the fire door or grate, which weighs just over a hundredweight, in line with what one would expect.

Not long afterwards we have a bill from Geo Wilding (but no mention of Willets) for more boiler plates. As this was about 20% of the original bill, Perhaps if this was the proportion of plates that needing replacing as matter of routine?

CHAPTER 2 References

1 J. Curr, *The Coal Viewer and Engine Builders Practical Companion* (Augustus M. Kelley, Reprinted 1970) ISBN 678051046.
2. S. Grudgings, The Lords of Westerleighs Colliery Works and Methods in the 1780s, *BIAS Journal 43*, p14.
3. S. Grudgings, The Coalpit Heath Coalfield: Developments in the Eighteenth Century, *BIAS Journal 42*, p52 .
4. J. Curr, Ref 1, p70.
5. Nottingham University Mi Av 179 1-69.

This 1758 coloured engraving by Francois Vivares showing the upper works at Coalbrookdale is particularly useful because in addition to giving a good view of the state of the works at that time it also indicates how Taylor's team of horses would have transported the cylinder to Coalpit Heath. The form of the cylinder is also clearly shown.

Reproduced by courtesy of Ironbridge Gorge Museums Trust

Mr. Charles Palmer

for the use of Colepitt bath
Fire Engion   To Ja.s Hilhouse &c.

1750		£		
Nov 15	To 77 Bars Iron	26. 1. 17 @ 16/	21. 2. 5½	
	To 2 B.rr Blister Steel	0. 1. 22 @ 27/	0. 12. 1	
	To 1 d.o German Steel	0. 0. 17 @ 6	0. 8. 6	
	To 2 Anvills	2. 2. 0 @ 40/	5. 0. 0	
	To 1 Vice	0. 1. 10½ @ 6	0. 19. 3	
	To 3 Stevens	0. 1. 4 @ 18/8	0. 5. 4	28. 7. 7½
Jany 9	To 81 Bars Iron	20. 2. 8 @ 16/6	16. 19. 5	
	To 2 Bars Shovel Iron	0. 3. 4 @ 17/	0. 13. 4	
	To 6 Br Tinton Rods	3. 0. 0 @ 25/	3. 15.	21. 7. 9
Feb 12	To 1 Pott	0. 1. 3 @ 16/4	0. 4. 6	
	To 2 Bars Iron	1. 1. 25 @ 17/6	1. 5. 10	
	To 3 Br best Tinton Rods	1. 2. 0 @ 27/	2. 0. 6	
	To 1 d.o drawn Rods	0. 2. 0 @ 21/	0. 10. 6	
	To 2 Bars Iron	0. 2. 26 @ 17/6	0. 12. 10	
19	To 12 Bars Iron	5. 1. 11 @ d.o	4. 13. 7	
21	To 1 door & frame & 1 damp Plat	4. 0. 21 @ 14/	2. 18. 7	
	To 1 B.rr Germ Steel	0. 0. 21 @ 53/	0. 9. 11	12. 16. 3
Mar 18	To 42 Bars Iron	10. 1. 20 @ 17/6	9. 2. 6	
	To 10 Bars Seberia Iron	3. 1. 16 @ 16/	2. 14. 3	
	To 1 Bar Spam Iron	0. 2. 5 @ 16/6	0. 9. 0	
	To 1 Br best Tinton Rods	0. 2. 0 @ 27/	0. 13. 6	12. 19. 3
1751				
July 8	To 2 Cylinders	4. 2. 13 @ 20/		4. 12. 4
			£	80. 3. 9½

1742
Rec.d of the Lords of the Mannor of
W.m Harleigh by Jacob Smith in full of the
above

For y.e use of Mr Ja.s Hilhouse Self &c.

Ja.s Getty

Palmers third bill for what the author has termed sundries.
Image Courtesy Manuscripts and Special Collections,
The University of Nottingham, Ref MiAv 171.5

Chapter 3
THE SUPPLIERS BILLS

3.1 Introduction

In Chapter 2 details from the suppliers bills have been used to establish the sequence of construction. This chapter is concerned with looking at each bill in detail, specifically the purpose of the items supplied, the background to the suppliers themselves as well as some of the technical considerations for the items they supplied and built.

The development of the Newcomen Engine as well as that of James Watts improvements to it is very much linked to (and to some extent determined by) the technological progress of the Iron Industry specifically:

- The replacement of charcoal with wood as a fuel for smelting Iron was developed and perfected by the Coalbrookdale Company and was one of the factors enabling progressive increases in hearth capacities. This development was instrumental in both reducing the cost of cast iron and enabling larger items to be produced.[1]
- The development of the tools and methods needed to bore cylinder, pipes and other large castings accurately in all dimensions, an area in which the Coalbrookdale company led the world for a while.[2]
- The development of new techniques for constructing heavy machinery in metal rather than wood, specifically which material to use for what purpose.

3.2 Origins and purpose of the bills

With the exception of Goldney's Account Book, all the bills examined originate from the LoW estate where careful record keeping and accounting appear to have been the norm. The reason for this is presumed to be so that allocations of costs and revenues between the three principals (Smith, Middleton and Colston) were clear and supported by documentation. Given that the partnership was relatively new and the partners geographically distant, this financial record keeping was particularly important. Expenditure on the LoW estate appears to have been split into separate Estate and Coal works accounts and in the latter there is a clear attempt to isolate and itemise the 'Fire Engine' bills.

There are two main sources for the bills and whilst there is some variation in the handwriting, the author's opinion is that most were transcribed or written up by the clerks to LoW from the submissions of the various suppliers.

Firstly the Bristol Records Office are custodians of the Ashton Court Papers, an extensive archive of materials relating to the Smythe Family of Ashton Court, into which Jarrit Smith married. There are many documents in this archive detailing the LoW coal mining activities, the majority dating from 18th century.

Secondly the Nottingham University Archives, are custodians of the Middleton papers, an ennobled family, resident at Wollaton near Nottingham. Their interests, of which coal mining was only part, were extensive and as a result this archive is also large and complex.

It has not been possible to locate any bills for the fire engine during this period in the Colston estate records.

3.3 Transcribing the materials

The bills enable the resources, sequences and duration of the construction and commissioning of the engine to be deduced with a high level of confidence. The bills have been, with a couple of exceptions, transcribed in full from the original documents. Original wording is denoted by italics and where uncertain, contained in square brackets.

Whilst the transcription process can be laborious, involving two people to maximise accuracy, it ensures a level of attention to content that a cursory read does not. It is fortunate that most of the writing is clear, our challenges have been:

- Interpretation of the terminology, some of which will be local, colloquial or technical, the meaning of which may have been lost over the intervening years.
- Interpretation of the weights, measures and currency of the time. Until 1971 the pound sterling was divided into twenty shillings, which were divided again into twelve pennies and denoted £sd. An imperial ton was divided into twenty hundredweights (cwts) each of four quarters (qtrs) of twenty eight pounds (lbs). Prices are usually quoted as shillings and pence per cwt or pence per lb.

Note: The calendar was reformed from the Julian to the Gregorian in September 1752 in Great Britain and the start of the year was officially changed from 25th March to Jan 1st, except for tax purposes. Although for many years prior to 1752, dual dating of year between Jan 1st and Mar 24th was used to avoid confusion. The materials are transcribed in verbatim, whilst the commentaries use the Gregorian calendar.

3.4 Charles Palmer's Bills

Charles Palmer appears to have been one of a family of local Engine Wrights, the known references to whom are listed in Appendix 2. Apparently commissioned by LoW to build the Engine, he appears to have filled the role that we would describe today as that of Project Engineer. Palmer is the central figure during the construction of the engine and house, his team of workmen apparently able to undertake a wide variety of tasks and duties. Palmer's purchase of the raw materials indicates he was recognised as having the requisite expertise in this area. If there is any doubt about the importance of his role, we only need look at his sundries bill which includes tips and drinks to a number of the workmen to recognise completion of some difficult work. Clearly he was the individual that the other suppliers answered to.

Understanding the nature of Palmers work and the basis of his expertise and others like him is, the author believes, central to understanding how the new technologies of the period (which the Newcomen engine was) were developed and deployed. It is thus suggested that Palmer was a self taught man, probably having learned his trade whilst working on mining machinery and also wind and water mills which needed similar skills. The existance of drawings would have been unlikely and tools would have been simple with knowledge being passed down from father to son and carefully protected.

Palmer presented three bills, for labour, materials and sundries given here as Sections 3.4.1, 3.4.2 and 3.4.3.

3.4.1 Charles Palmer's Bill for Labour (Nottingham University Ref. Mi Av 171/4)

This is the longest bill of all and because of this has not been transcribed. The bill runs from 27th October 1750 to 13th March 1752 and represents 1,030¼ man days of labour. It would appear that Palmer's men have responsibility for constructing and finishing not only the engine and boiler but its house and the pitwork as well. The main features of note are:

- Palmer accounts for his own and his men's time on a weekly basis and the levels of these charges are shown in the table below.
- Palmer's daily charge was 2s 8d with his men charged at 1s 6d or 8d.
- There appears to be a regular team of five men, James Rogers, Edward Cowles, Joseph Moone, James Lane and Giles Ball who work with him from November 1750 through to April 1751. These five are joined for short periods by individuals whose suggested specialisms are bracketed (based on the work underway at the time of their employment). Joseph Price (construction of the beam?) William Skinner and John Farmer (both heavy lifting specialists?) and Aaron Hardman (lead or boiler work).
- At his team's busiest period in the week of 26th January 1751, Palmer bills for himself and seven others.
- By April only four of Palmer's team are involved but all appear to be working round the clock, presumably to get the engine working.
- From June 1751 Palmer's bills become less regular and include a higher proportion of his personal time. Probably for fine tuning and supervising the permanent engine men.
- Training the enginemen would have been a challenge for Palmer and LoW, as men with previous experience would be hard to find and responsibility for machinery of this value would not be handed over lightly.

- The total of Palmer's first bill is £114 14s 6d and this is noted as being settled (minus the final 6d, as appears to have been Jarrit's custom) on 29th August 1752.
- The above figure includes an amount of £20 described as '*you promised to pay me over and above my daily wages the sum of 20 pounds for directing the fire engine*'.

3.4.2 Palmer's Bill for Iron and Steel (Nottingham University Ref. MI Av 168/39)

Mr. Charles Palmer
For the use of Colepit Heath
Fire Engion   For Jas Hillhouse [Co]

		c q l		£ s d
1750				
Nov 15	To 77 Barrs Iron	26-1-17	@16/	21. 2. 5½
	To 2 Brs Blister Steel	0-1-22	@27/	0.12. 1
	To 1 do German Steel	0-0-17	@6	0. 8. 6
	To 2 Anvills	2-2- 0	@40/	5. 0. 0
	To 1 Vice	0-1-10½	@6	0.19. 3
	To 3 Shevers	0-1- 4	@18/8	0. 5. 4
Jan 9	To 81 Barrs Iron	20-2- 8	@16/6	16.19. 5
	To 2 [Dozen] Shovels Iron	0-3- 4	17/	0.13. 4
	To 6 Brs Linton Rods	3-0- 0	25/	3.15. 0
Feb 12	To 1 [Pot]	0-1- 3	16/4	0. 4. 6
	To 2 Barrs Iron	1-1-25	17/6	1. 5.10
	To 3 Brs best Linton Rods	1-2- 0	27/	2. 0. 6
	To 1 do [drawn] Rods	0-2- 0	21/	0.10. 6
	To 2 Barrs Iron	0-2-26	17/6	0.12.10
19	To 12 Barrs Iron	5-1-11	do	4.13. 7
21	To 1 dose & [_ame] damp Plate	4-0-21	14/	2.18. 7
	To 1 Barr German Steel	0-0-21	53/	0. 9.11
Mar 18	To 42 Barrs Iron	10-1-20	17/6	9. 2. 6
	To 10 Barrs Soberial Iron	3-1-16	16/	2.14. 3
	To 1 Barr Span Iron	0-2- 5	16/6	0. 9. 0
	To 1 Brs best Linton Rods	0-2- 0	27/	0.13. 6
1751				
July 13	To 2 Cylinders	4-2-13	20/	4.12. 4
				80. 3. 2½

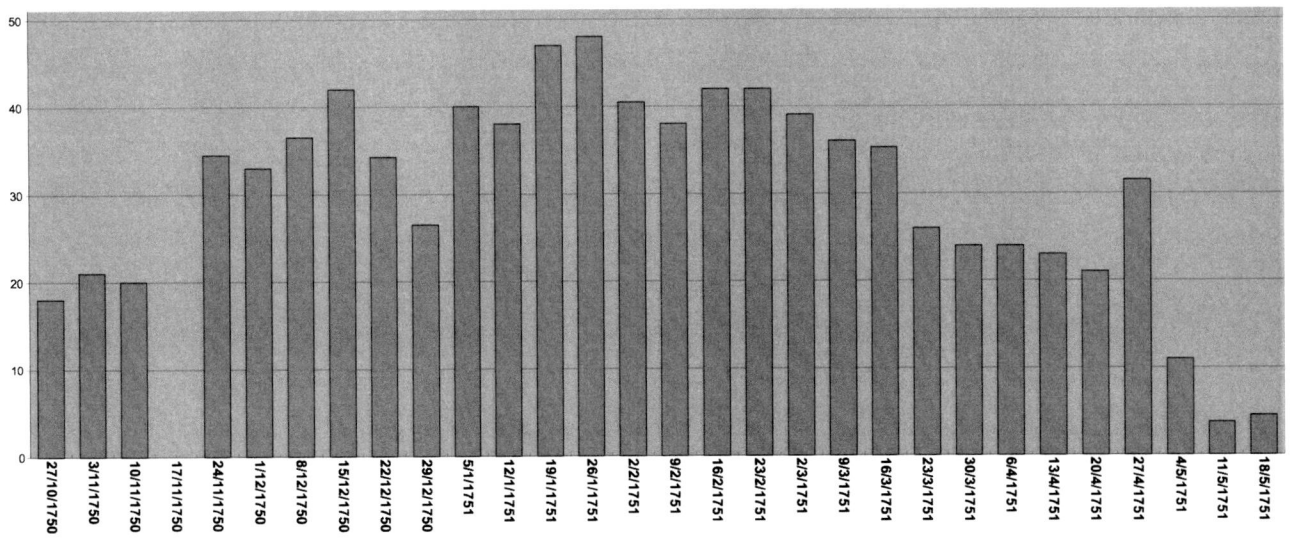

Palmers Labour Bill Breakdown

Commentary on Palmer's Iron and Steel Bill

This bill includes a number of different types of Iron and Steel which with research, give some insight into the state of the domestic iron industry at the midpoint of the 18th century. From the early part of the century this country's domestic production had not been able to keep up with the increasing demand and the Basque part of Spain initially supplied much of the shortfall. It was the inability of the Basque sources to respond to the continuing growth in UK demand that opened the door for imports of Swedish Iron. These developed to the point that by 1720, imports from Sweden were running at 15,000 tons, roughly equal to the levels of domestic production. By 1750, Russian iron, had also secured a sizeable share of this countries market.[3]

Because of Bristol's position, it was the main port on this country's western seaboard for Iron imports and supplied much of the western midlands and border counties via the River Severn. By the end of the century Great Britain was self sufficient in basic iron, mostly as a result of the development of large scale ironmaking in South Wales, Central Scotland and elsewhere and Bristol's importance in this trade diminished.

The phrase 'For ye use of Hilhouse Self and Co - Jas Getty' at the head of this bill suggests the involvement of Hillhouse and Co, who RR Angerstein, an industrial observer from Sweden describes in June 1754 during his sojourn in Bristol as 'The principal foundry belongs to Mr Hillhouse and Co who also own a forge where anvils, hammers, ships requisites and small anchors are made'.[4] By 1773 Hillhouse had started building ships near Hotwells Rd, the business eventually developing into Charles Hill and Co in 1845, launching their last ship in 1976.[5]

Getty is understood to be a misspelling for Getley whose name appears on bills later in the sequence and whose trade is given as Ironmonger in his will.[6] Hillhouse Getley and Co were Bristol iron merchants who owned the Welch foundry there as well as a blast furnace at Neath. They later became Reynolds, Getley and Co and owned other Ironworks.[7]

It appears therefore, that Palmer sub contracted or fronted Hillhouse's billing for different types and grades of iron and steel presumably to control costs and ensure that the smiths were using appropriate materials. He may also have made his own mark up on them too.

Palmer's materials bill is nearly concurrent with Arthers' and in the absence of separate materials bills from Arthers, his blacksmiths are assumed to have used materials supplied by Palmer. The categories of materials are not all clear but the author's interpretations are as follows:

- Blister steel – although bulk production of steel did not commence for another century, small scale production of steel had been underway for some time. This method of production in which often Swedish but sometimes Russian or Spanish bar Iron was converted in a cementation furnace, resulted in a blistered surface which prompted this name.[8] Blister steel was not a homogenous product and needed further forging or smithing before use. This challenge of producing steel of a consistent quality was not resolved until the Huntsman process of making crucible steel was popularised later in the century.

- German Steel – high quality forged steel. Sourced either from Germany, where it was made by direct smelting, or more likely from the main domestic supplier, William Bertram in the North East[9] where it was made by repeated piling and forging of blister steel. Angerstein describes a steel works at Keynsham operated by the Shallard Family, located next to the Brass Mills where Iron was converted to steel for a charge per ton[10] so this is a third possibility. Its price of twice that of blister steel presumably being due to the amount of processing it needed.

- Shovel Iron – probably being iron of a section and form suitable for shovel blades.[11]

- Spans Iron – this is likely to be Spanish Iron.[12]

- Soberial Iron – this is most likely to be Siberian Iron – apparently its journey overland from the forge took up to two years.[13]

- Barrs of Iron – basic cast iron, used for general purposes by the smiths. Swedish Iron was generally recognised as the better quality, but domestically produced bars were also used. The weights of the *barr*s appear to differ slightly between consignments indicating the non standardized way in which they were made.

- Linton Rods – this has puzzled everyone, the best current guess is that it originated from an Ironworks at Linton on the Gloucs/Herefordshire border. However as it is understood to have closed by 1692 this remains conjectural.[14] Palmer obviously needed lots of these rods, whatever they were.

3.4.3 Palmer's Sundries Bill, adjusted to sequential dates (Nottingham University Ref. Mi Av 171/5)

Charles Palmer's 2nd Bill Copied

		£	s	d
1750				
Novry 17th	Paid to Benjamin Butter			
	To 1 pair Smiths Bellows	2.	10.	0
	To 1 pair ditto	2.	5.	0
27th	Paid Mr Evans			
	To 6 large 28 foot flat [uffors] at 5	1.	10.	0
	To 3 Round White Spars at 16	2.	8.	0
Decemb 24	Paid Mr Evans for Deals	3.	9.	9
Jany 24	Paid Mr Matthews for loading the Cilleder & Bottom	0.	10.	1
Feby 23rd	Paid to Timothy Cook for Files	0.	4.	7
	Paid to Timothy Cook for Files	0.	5.	7
	Paid to Mr Elton for Sturbridge Clay	1.	0.	0
	Paid Abraham Williams for going to Framilode 4 Times & twice to Coalbrook Deal	1.	10.	0
March 18th	Paid Mr Fry for 2 yards of Nap	0.	2.	4
	Ditto for Blanketing	0.	6.	0
1751				
April 12	Paid Mr Pidding for Leather Straps	0.	15.	0
Febry 9	Paid Mr Evans for Deal	4.	19.	0
19	Paid Mr Jones for Sturbridge Bricks	4.	4.	0
Janry 5	Gave Mr Arthurs Smiths to drink	0.	1.	0

		£ s d
22nd	Gave to Trowman	0. 1. 0
24th	Gave to ye Porter for bringing Goods from the Key to Lawford's Gate	0. 0. 6
Febry 6	Gave Mr Arthur Smith	0. 0. 6
	Gave Edwd [Cowles] for going to Framilow	0. 2. 6
19	Gave the Iron Foundry	0. 1. 0
	Gave Mr Arthur Smith	0. 0. 6
March 5	Gave the Porter for loading Sturbridge	0. 0. 6
April 5	Gave the Porters for loading 2 Waggons wth Iron	0. 4. 6
	Gave the Hallier for halling of Pipes from the Key to Lawford's Gate	0. 2. 6
8	Gave the Hallier for halling the Cistern & Buckets to Lawford's Gate	0. 2. 0
	Gave the Smiths	0. 1. 0
19	Gave the Porters for loading a Waggon	0. 2. 0
	-- -- -- for loading 2 Waggons	0. 4. 0
	To 1 Tarr Brush	0. 0. 6
	For loading the Boiler Top	0. 1. 6
		£27. 4.10

Commentary on Palmer's Sundries Bill

This bill, correlates nicely with many of the entries by other suppliers and enables cross referencing with their bills. Some specific entries worthy of mention include:

- On Nov 27th, Dec 24th and February 9th Palmer makes payments for deal (understood to be planks) and other types of wood to Messrs Evans, it is suggested this was for applications such as scaffolding, door frames and roofing timbers The purpose of the '28 foot [offers]' and 'round white spars' have been suggested in Chapter 2 as being for the beam and the sheerlegs respectively.
- His tips to the trowmen, smiths and iron foundry presumably recognise successful completion of difficult pieces of work and reinforce the view that Palmer held overall responsibility for the project and the suppliers were answerable to him.
- The various trips to Framilode and Coalbrookdale are presumed to be to place additional orders and/or describe the materials requirements in detail.
- It is interesting to see the well known local name of Elton[15] being paid for Stourbridge Clay on 23rd February, presumably they were either agents or had a ready supply of it.
- 'Two Yards of Nap' and 'Blanketing' are difficult to place, possibly for insulation or lagging steam pipes or protective clothing for the men working in the shaft.
- The leather straps charged in April 12th may be hinges or gaskets for the clack doors. In later years it was found that Hippopotamus leather was the most suitable for this purpose.[16]

3.5 Robert Taylor's Haulage Bill
(Nottingham Univ. Ref Mi Av 168/43)

Oct'br ye 29th 1750 – To Jarrit Smith and Comp' D'r to Robert Taylor for Work done by his Plow for ye use of ye Fire Engine

Date		£ s d
Oct Ye 29	To a Days Work Halling Lime	0.10. 0
30th	To a Days Work Halling Timber	0. 8. 6
31st	To Do	0. 8. 6
Nov ye 1st	To Do	0. 8. 6
2nd	To a Days Work Halling Sand	0. 7. 0
6th	To a Days Work Halling Timber	0. 8. 6
7th	To Do for Stones	0. 7. 0
8th	To Do	0. 7. 0
9th	To Do	0. 7. 0
12th	To Do	0. 7. 0
13th	To Do	0. 7. 0
14th	To Do	0. 7. 0
15th	To a Days Work Halling Timber	0. 8. 6
16th	To Do Stones	0. 7. 1
19th	To a Days Work to Bristol for Brick	0.11. 0
20th	To Do	0.11. 0
21st	To Days Work Halling Stones	0. 7. 0
22nd	To Do	0. 7. 0
23rd	To Do	0. 7. 0
26th	To a Days Work to Bristol for Brick	0.11. 0
27th	To Do for Stones	0. 6. 6
28th	To Do	0. 7. 0
29th	To Do	0. 7. 0
30th	To a Days Work Halling Timber	0. 7. 0
Dec ye 1st	To a Days Work to Bristol for Brick	0.11. 0
5th	To Do for Timber	0. 8. 6
6th	To Do	0. 8. 6
7th	To Do	0. 8. 6
8th	To Do	0. 8. 6
9th	To Do	0. 8. 6
17th	To a Days Work Halling Stones	0. 7. 0
18th	To a Days Work to Bristol for Brick	0.11. 0
19th	To a Days Work Halling Stones	0. 7. 0
20th	To a Days Work to Bristol for Brick	0.11. 0
21st	To Do for Stones	0. 7. 0
22d	To a Days Work to Bristol for Brick	0.11. 0
27th	To a Days Work Halling Stones	0. 7. 0
28th	To Do	0. 7. 0
29th	To Do	0. 7. 0
31st	To a Days Work Halling Timber	0. 8. 6
Jan ye 1st	To Do	0. 8. 6
2nd	To a Days Work to Bristol for Brick	0.11. 0
3rd	To Do for Timber	0. 8. 6
4th	To a Days Work to Bristol for Brick	0.11. 0
5th	To Do for Timber	0. 8. 6
7th	To Days Work to Bristol for Brick	0.11. 0
8th	To a Days Work Halling Stones	0. 7. 0
9th	To a Days Work to Bristol for Iron	0.11. 0
10th	To a Days Work Halling Stones	0. 7. 0
11th	To Do	0.10. 0
Jan 12th	To Do	0.10. 0
14th	To Do	0. 7. 0
15th	To Do	0. 7. 0
16th	To a Days Work to Bristol for Brick	0.11. 0
17th	To Do	0.11. 0
18th	To Do for Timber	0. 8. 6
19th	To Do	0. 8. 6

Date		£ s d
21st	To Do for Stones	0. 7. 0
22nd	To Days Work Halling Timber	0. 8. 6
23rd	To Do for Stones	0. 7. 0
24th	To Days Work to Bristol for Sundrys	0.11. 0
25th	To Do Stones	0. 7. 0
26th	To a Days Work to Bristol for Ye Bottom of Ye Cylinder	0.11. 0
28th	To Do for Stones	0. 7. 0
29th	To Do for Timber	0. 8. 6
30th	To a Days Work to Bristol for Brick	0.11. 0
31st	To Do for Stones	0. 8. 0
Feb ye 1st	To a Days Work to Bristol for Lead	0.11. 0
2nd	To Do	0.11. 0
4th	To Do	0.11. 0
5th	To Do	0.11. 0
6th	To Do	0.11. 0
7th	To Do	0.11. 0
8th	To Do	0.11. 0
9th	To Do	0.11. 0
11th	To Do	0 11 0
12th	To Do	0.11. 0
19th	To Do	0.11. 0
25th	To Days Work Halling Stones	0.11. 0
27th	To Do	0.10.. 0
28th	To Do	0. 7. 0
March 1st	To a Days Work to Bristol for Brick	0.11. 0
2nd	To Do Stones	0. 7. 0
4th	To Do	0. 7. 0
6th	To Do	0. 7. 0
7th	To a Days Work to Bristol for Brick	0.11. 0
13th	To a Days Work to Bristol for Brick	0.11. 0
14th	To Do for Stones	0. 7. 0
15th	To Do	0. 7. 0
April 13th	To a Days Work to Bristol for Pump Barrels	0.11. 0
May 15th	To Do	0.11. 0
16th	To Do	0.11. 0
17th	To a Days Work Halling Stones	0. 7. 0
18th	To Do	0. 7. 0
19th	To a Days Work Halling Timber	0. 8. 6
21st	To Do	0. 8. 6
22nd	To Do	0. 8. 6
	Total £42.16. 6	

1750 9th of February Rec'd of Mr Abraham Highnham in part of the above Bill   10. 0

Commentary on Taylor's Haulage Bill

Taylor appears to be a general haulier, providing teams of horses, handling deliveries of coal both locally and into Bristol as well as supplying straw. His bill appears to cover most of the heavy haulage of items needed to build and commission the engine. The term 'plow' is a contemporary term for a team of animals harnessed to a wagon.

The bulk of November's entries are for stone with the occasional load of brick, sand and lime, exactly what would be expected in the early stages of construction. The LoW are understood to have operated their own brickworks and quarries so it is a reasonable assumption that these items were supplied by the estate. The quantities of timber suggest it was used for scaffolding and again possibly estate sourced.

Highnam appears to be responsible for managing the estates finances as his name appears frequently when payments are being made.

There is a further bill from Robert Taylor held in the BRO under reference AC/AS/97/3 which includes entries for 'five days work at the engine' between 11th to 16th December 1750 and a nights work on the 10th. The author interprets this as the use of Taylor's horses to provide power on the engine site, possibly for raising and locating heavy stone (probably the massive one piece engine bedstones that would weigh over a ton each) rather than haulage. This bill is not included here, nor is not referred to in any of the accounts or summaries, possibly because only a small proportion related to the Engine.

3.6 James Malcott's Brasswork Bill
(Nottingham University Ref. Mi Av 168/69)

Jarratt Smith Esq & Comp

To James Malcott Dr

1750		c q l		£ s d
Decm 11	8 Shivers qt	0-2- 0	at 12	2.16. 0
Febry 5	2 Large Brasses qt	1-1-15	at 12	7.15. 0
13	2 Valves qt	0-0- 7	at 16	0. 9. 4
March 11	a Regulater and other work	3-1-13	at 16	25. 2. 8
11	2 Brasses qt	0-0-19½	at 12	0.19. 3
	A Basket & [Hollier]			0. 2. 0
1751				
June 6	3 Brasses qt	0-0- 3	10oz	0. 3. 7½
				37. 7.10½

Commentary on Malcott's Bill

Given that Bristol was this country's main centre of brass making there would presumably have been a number of merchants specialising in this material. Malcott is known to have supplied similar materials to John Wise in 1742 for the Chelsea waterworks engine[17] so it is possible he also supplied brasswork for the three Bristol engines we know were built by Wise in the later 1730s. Malcott was wealthy and important enough to put in place a £300 bond with the City of Bristol in 1759.[18] He died in 1761.[19]

The items supplied appear to be brass fittings needed as the work progresses. Brass is an easier material to cast as it is molten at a lower temperature than iron and used where finer tolerances and greater accuracy are needed. The cost of the 'reguleter' at £25 is a significant expense and the ability to cast a regulator housing indicates a high level of skill.

3.7 Nathaniel Arthers's Bill for Blackmith work
(Nottingham University Ref MI Av 168/40)

Jarrett Smith Esq

To Nathl. Arthers Dr

1750		c q l	£ s d
Dec 5th	To One New Sledge 19½ lbs @ 6d		0. 9. 9
10th	To One New Vice 1-0-3 @7½		3.11. 10½
	To One Screw Plate and Tapps	0-0-[9]	1. 1. 0
	Two Chains	6-1- 6	

		c q l	£ s d
	2 Bridles and Nutts	0-0- 8	
	One [Bore] for the Piston & [Braces] & Nutts	2-2-17	
	Drilling & Cutting 4 New Holes in the Piston for the [Braces], Chipping the main hole		
	Cutting 10 holes Square & Boring for the [Braces] & filling the Bore		1.14. 0
Jan 16th	To One Balance Beam Gudgeon	2-2-25	
26th	To One Chain	2-1-07	
	One Bridle and Nutts	0-0-03½	
	One Damper Gudgeon	0-1-01¾	
Feb 19th	To a Piston Stem & 2 Brass & Nutts	2-2-17½	
	To 2 Chains	6-1- 6	
	To 10 Screw Bolts & Nutts for ye Piston	0-1-16	
	To 3 Hooks and 3 Staples for ye Bore	1-1-26	
23rd	To Iron Work for 2 pairs of Bucketts 4 pairs Flaps & 8 Screw Bolts	0-0-10½	
	To One Bottom Buckett & Daggers wth [4.T __] one Dagger	0-1- 6	
Mar 5th	To One Chain	2-1-15½	
	To One Bridle	0-0- 4	
11th	To a Small Chain	0-1-2¾	
1751 Apl 12th	To 8 Screw Brace and Nutts for 2 plugs for the Door Side	1-0-26½	
	To Chipping the Holes in the Cast Iron		0.15. 0
	To Iron Works for 6 Small Bucketts one Long Rod wth 2 pairs of Joynts and Daggers	1-2-23½	
	To Single Joynt & Daggers & 3 Bolts	0-1-26	
	To 12 pair of Flaps & 12 Screw Bolts	0-0-24½	
	To Iron Works for 4 Large Bucketts & Dagers & 2 Bolts & Daggers	1-0- 6	
	To 8 pair of Flaps & 16 Screw Bolts	0-1-24½	
	To One Small Chain	0-2- 2	
	To 2 Rodd Capps and Joynts	2-1-15½	
	To 2 Single Joynts & Dagers & 2 Bottom Daggers	0-3-26	
	To 11 Screw Bolts and Nutts	0-0- 9½	
May 1st	To 1 Single Joynt and Hoop	0-0- 4¼	
		37-1-24¾ @4¾d	83. 1. 2½
			90.12.10

Denis Diderot produced a superb set of engravings of the leading technical processes of the time that was published in 1751/2. This image, whilst showing a roomier and tidier forge than might be expected does show the main processes and tools that Arthers' men would have been using on the engine site.

Commentary on Arthers' Bill

The smith's work was of vital importance as they produced the individual components as well as all the strapping, links, screws, bolts, cotters and such like that held the whole mechanism together. They would have needed a good understanding of what iron and steel to use, its strength under tension and compression as well as its hardness and the likely wear rates. Until this period large scale machinery had always been made in wood and examination of early metal assemblies shows the application of classic carpentry techniques to linking and joining metal assemblies.[20] As casting and machining capabilities improved over time such smithed assemblies were superseded by machined castings and forgings.

It has not been possible to discover anything more about Arthers and the author assumes that he was a well established local smith capable of fielding a skilled team. The bills indicate that Arthers' team did the smithing work on both engine and pitwork and remained on site until just before the engine was operational. Arthers and his men returned in the following years, indicating both the importance of their work and their good relationship with LoW.

Examination of the few remaining examples and images of smithed components used on Newcomen engine[23] shows a wide variation in methods and approaches and whilst this is to be expected, it does not help inform how Arthers' men worked. However, we can learn the following from Arthers' bill:

- The bills start on 5th December 1750 with a charge for a vice and a sledge (hammer?), it is interesting that Palmer rather than Arthers supplied the anvils and bellows.
- It is suspected the work on 'filling the bore' is filing by hand of the cylinder to ensure a consistent fit with the piston.
- The bill of £6 1s 6d for two chains in December 1750 is thought to be for the large chains made up of multiple links (like a huge bicycle chain) which connect the ends of the beam to the pump rods and piston. It is not clear whether the individual links were cast or forged, given that this is Smiths work, the latter is assumed. Arthers' men would have forged the link pins and assembled the chains, hence the cost. They produced a further chain in late January and another pair in mid February and a final one in early March.

A repaired wrought iron link from the chains suspended from both ends of the Pentrich Engine beam. Wear on the links must have been significant and breakages regular, presumably being repaired by the resident pit blacksmith when the engine was not working.

This complete cast iron link was found on the site of the 1791 Serridge engine and probably indicates a trend towards using cast rather than wrought iron links. This is presumed to be because of the progressive reduction in the cost of cast iron and also the advantage of the larger bearing section being able to accommodate greater wear. It measures approximately 13in. x 5in. x 1³/₄in. and weighs 20lb.

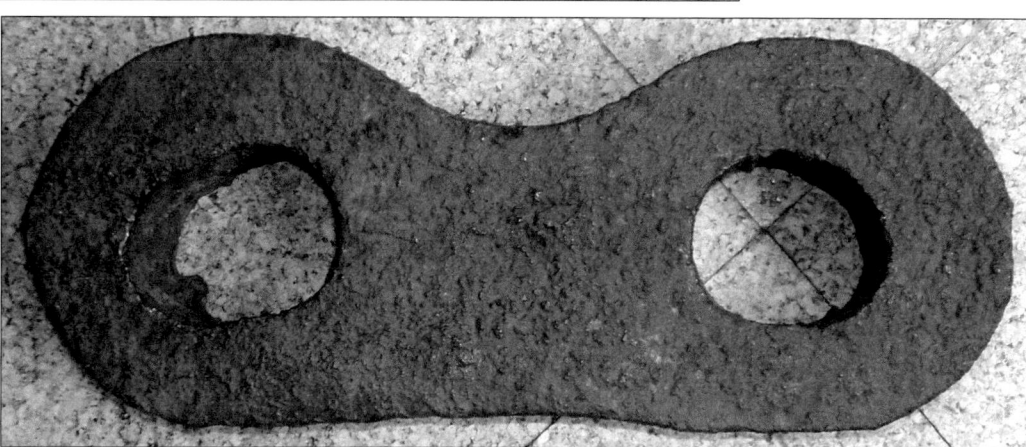

This image of the indoor end of the South Liberty engine beam from the 1895 *Engineering* report gives some idea of the bulk of the beam as well as the complexity of all the wrought iron strapping and braces that secures it. This massive weight would pivot on the balance beam gudgeon produced by Arthers' men in January and its unfortunate that the South Liberty gudgeon is not visible in this image.

- Arthurs' men needed to make the piston stem (rod) and they billed for this on 19th February. Once made it needed fitting securely to the piston plate. It is not known how they did this but the method apparently used on the Pentrich engine was to insert a tapered cotter pin through the cast socket in the piston plate into a corresponding slot in the end of the piston stem. The entry for '*drilling and cutting 4 new holes in the piston for the [braces] and chipping the main hole*' suggests the piston plate did not have a socket cast in (probably being beyond Coalbrookdale's mould making capabilities) and that the stem was secured to the piston plate by braces or straps (see also frontis for Smeaton's plans of pistons).

- It is believed that the '*10 screw bolts and nutts for ye piston*' on 19th February would be to locate and retain the piston ring and enable it to be tightened into position against the piston plate to secure the materials used to provide the seal between piston and cylinder walls (see also 3.7).

- Arthurs' Bill makes no obvious reference to the flexible joint or cross head between the end of the piston rod and the chains. This was one of those vital connections through which the power of the engine was transmitted. The illustrations of the equivalent joint on the Pentrich engine (see also 3.7) show one of approaches to making such a joint.

- On February 23rd there is an entry for '*Iron Work for 2 pairs of buckets and 4 pairs of flaps and 8 screw bolts*' – It is believed that this is for fitting the internals for the pump rods.

- On April 12th there are charges for work on buckets and joints and daggers as well as '*chipping the holes in the cast iron*' – it appears that most of April's work was concerned with pitwork, specifically installing the clacks, clack doors and buckets within the barrels. It is suggested that '*daggers*' are early smithed cotter pins, tapered like a dagger to facilitate fitting and adjustment.

Right: The piston stem would need to be a high quality forging because of all the stresses placed on it. The Pentrich engine stem appears to be secured in the socket on the piston plate by a tapered cotter, presumably additional fixings were also required but these are not visible. Note also the six retaining bolts to secure the top flange to the piston. The top flange also has hoops built into it, probably to facilitate the frequent removal required when the soft sealing material sandwiched between flange and piston plate needed replacing to minimise air and water leaks.

Left: This image of the top of the Elsecar cylinder and piston show that a similar set of radial flanges were cast into this piston plate too. The slight flaring of the cylinder mouth is visible too.

Left and above: These images of the Pentrich engine connection between piston stem and chains show how this arrangement was designed and executed. It's not known if this was the original arrangement but if so it seems to have served well, being in regular use for over 120 years.

A simple cotter on the Pentrich engine, but hand made to fit.

3.8 Thomas Goldney's Bill for Castings from Coalbrookdale
(Nottingham University Ref MI Av168/41)

Jarrett Smith Esqr & Companies Dr to Thos Goldney & Co:-
For Fire Engine and Castings as follows.

		c q l		£ s d
1750				
Janry 21	A 42 Inc Cylinder bored	54-1- 7		
	A Bottom to it	15-3-14		
	A Jack-head Pipe, bored	3-3- 9		
		74-0- 2	@30s	111. 0. 6¼
	A Piston Plate	7-3- 7	@12s	4.13. 9
				115. 4. 3¼
Febry 5	A 6 foot Pipe, bored, 8½ in diam	4-1- 0		
	8 Buckets	0-3-13		
		5-0-13	@30s	7.13. 5¾
1751				
Aprl 6	2 Working Barrells 9 ft long, 12 inches diameter, bored	18-0-26		
	1 Sinking Pipe	4-0-24		
		22-1-22	@30s	3.13. 4½
22	Pitt Barrells	156-0-24	@18s	140.11.10¼
	8 Buckets & Clacks	2-1-14	@30s	3.11. 3
	2 Clack Doors	4-1- 0	@14s	2.19. 6
	1 Brass Clack	0-1-16½	@1s4dlb	2.19. 4
				183.15. 3¾
				307. 3. 0¾

Commentary on Goldney's Bill

Goldney's activities in the supply of iron castings and his links with the Coalbrookdale Company are described in Ken Rogers book[21] and the history of the Goldney dynasty is set out in Peter Stembridge's books[22] so only a summary of both is given here.

Thomas Goldney III (1694-1768) was a Bristol Merchant and Banker, son and grandson of previous Thomas Goldneys who had been prominent citizens of Bristol since the mid 17th Century. They were part of the local community of Quaker industrialists[23] and Thomas (II) invested in fellow Quaker Abraham Darby's Bristol Ironworks. The family connection was sustained after Darby relocated his operation up the Severn to Coalbrookdale,[24] owning $^{11}/_{16}$th of the company. Thomas (III) and his father both apparently acted as agent for the Coalbrookdale company, appearing to have the sole agency for Wales and the Southwest of England..[25]

Newcomen cylinders were initially cast in brass, a more expensive material but easier to work, the cost advantages of Iron became more compelling as cylinder sizes increased. Abraham Darby's Coalbrookdale company developed a reputation as the leading foundry for casting and boring such cylinders in iron until the entry of the Scottish Carron company and John Wilkinson of Bersham into this market in the 1760s.

This cylinder (42-inch diameter and nearly three tons weight) was a bored sleeve of cast iron and the first challenge was to smelt sufficient metal in a single batch to cast it. This needed a suitably large casting floor and sufficient furnace and hearth capacity to be confident of producing over three tons of iron in one 'blast', plus of course the capability to make moulds that were sufficiently large and stable. Once successfully cast, the next challenge was to bore the cylinder accurately in all dimensions. The ability to both cast and bore on this scale was very much at the leading edge of the technology of the time.

The details of this bill are duplicated in the Goldney account book held in the Wiltshire & Swindon History Centre.[26] This book contains the additional detail that the cylinder was shipped *off Beards Trow*. 'Trow' being the local term for the flat bottomed sailing vessels that carried merchandise up and down the Severn from Shrewsbury down to the Bristol Channel, only going out

'Trow' is the term used for the flat bottomed sailing boats that plied the River Seven from Shrewsbury to the Bristol Channel. One is seen here under full sail. *Nash*, **History of Worcestershire, 1781**

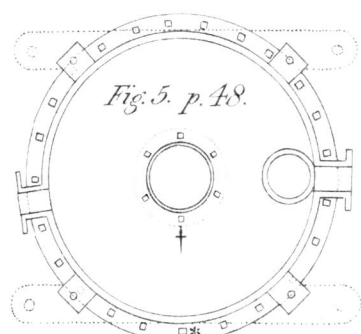

The entry in Goldney's account book for the Cylinder of the 1751 engine.

Image reproduced by courtesy WRO

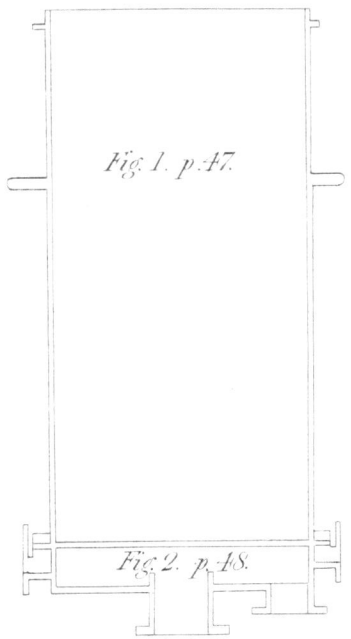

Fig. 1. p. 47.

Fig. 2. p. 48.

Fig. 5. p. 48.

Left: Currs cylinder plan and section does not reveal any particular surprises. Given the 40 year gap between the 1751 engine and Currs book, the technology for casting and boring of cylinders would be expected to have improved significantly as the number of cast in flanges, lugs and junctions suggest.

Below: We are fortunate that when R. R. Angerstein visited Coalbrookdale in 1754 in addition to describing how cylinders were bored he also sketched the process. He reported that the cylinder (a) was placed on a specially constructed carriage travelling on a track, drawn toward a rotating cutting head (b). The drive shaft for the cutting head is securely located between two mounts, the one nearest the cylinder being secured to the travelling carriage (d) and the other fixed (e). In this way the centring of both cylinder and cutting wheel could be controlled. Angerstein reported that this process needed several passes as heavy cuts were not possible and that the process could be carried out in 8-14 days by one man. The implication being that this was faster/ and or less labour intensive than previous methods. *Image Reproduced by courtesy of Peter Berg*

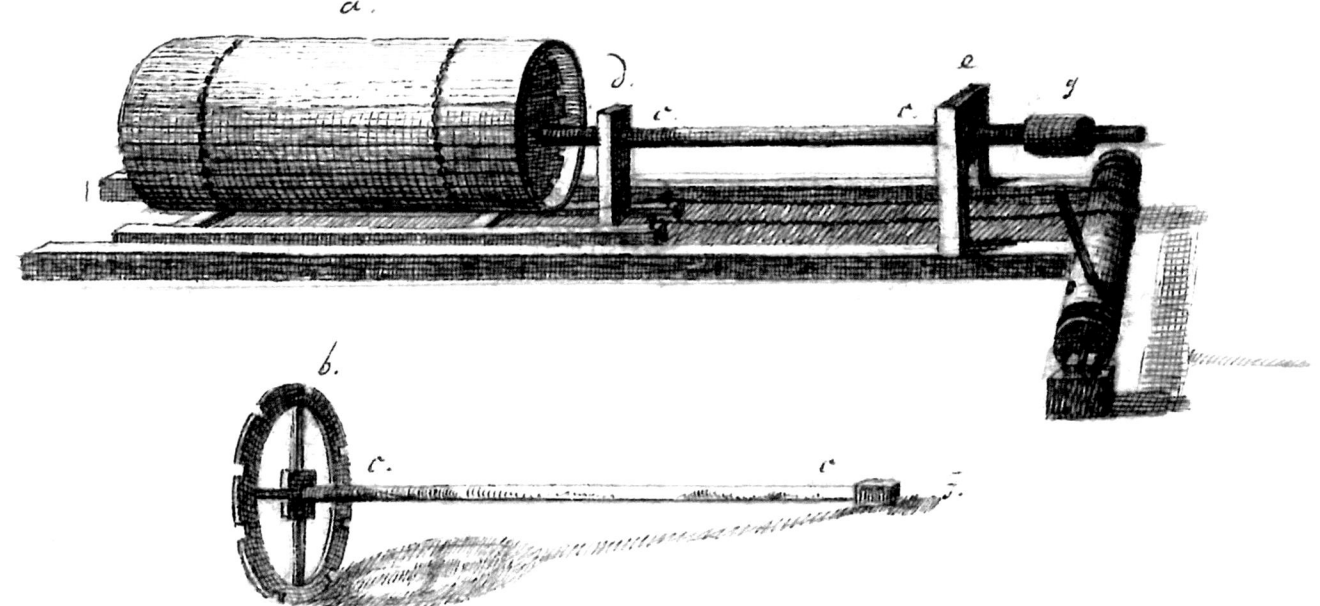

of use in the last century. Beard is presumed to be Eustace Beard who appears to have been a regular and trusted carrier for the Coalbrookdale company at this time.[27]

Note the difference in price between items than needed to be bored such as the cylinder, buckets and clacks, charged at 30s per hundredweight and those that did not such as the piston plate charged at 12s per hundredweight. There are also items such as working barrels, pit barrels and clack doors priced at levels between these two extremes. The price differentials are understood to reflect the differing levels of finishing work done on the castings.

Other components listed include:

- The 'bottom' – in effect a conical base, intended to be bolted underneath the cylinder, presumably to provide additional reinforcement and mounting points for the cylinder.

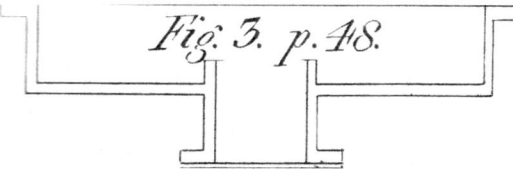

This section of the cylinder bottom from Curr gives some idea of the arrangements used 40 years later.

- The 'piston plate' – a cast round plate, just under 42-inches diameter and weighing over a third of a ton. When fitted with a crosshead bearing to the stem or connecting rod, the vacuum in the cylinder acted on this plate, moving it downwards to provide the power stoke.

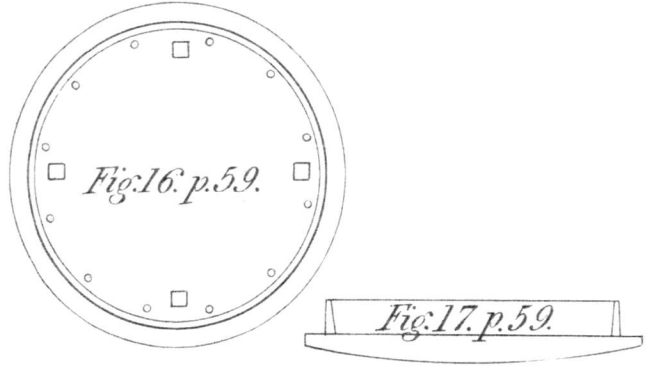

Curr's plan and section of the Piston plate confirms the simple form of this large circle of cast iron.

The arrangements needed to secure the piston flange retaining bolts in the body of the Pentrich piston plate are shown here. The gap between the piston plate and the top flange would be filled with the materials used for the seal and the retaining bolts would be progressively tightened as this wore out to maintain the effectiveness of the seal. The arrangements on the 1751 engine are expected to be similar. The nut, bolt, cotter and washers in this image appear to be all blacksmith made.

One of the challenges faced by Palmer and others like him was how to make an effective seal between piston and cylinder wall. The general practice appears to have been to use an iron ring the same diameter as the piston and secured to it and fill the gap with a combination of hemp, rope, dung and grease that would be flexible enough to make the seal but strong enough not to wear away immediately.

The buckets, pipes and pit barrels were delivered from April onwards when the pit work was being installed and clacks and clack doors would have been fitted at the same time. It is suspected that the entry in Arthers' bill for chipping the holes in the cast iron on April 12 was for cutting the clack door apertures in the pipes (by a mix of hand drilling and chisel work). Iron moulding technology not being advanced enough to cast them in. These doors were needed to provide access to the piston and clacks to enable replacement of the clack seals and hinges, the items subject to the greatest wear.

It is noted that Goldney, rather than Malcott, supplied a brass clack and it would be interesting to understand why it was made in this material and where it was used. Given that Goldney was a partner in the Warmley copper and brass works it is probable that this was its source.

Finally it would appear (on this and all other bills) that Jarrit Smith settled the bill on behalf of the LOW with a credit period of seven months being the norm.

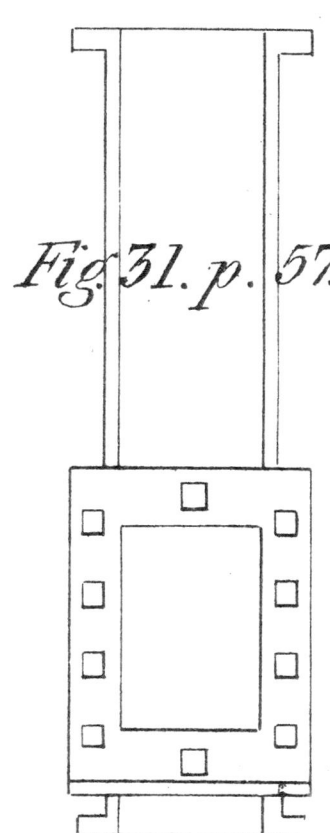

This image from Curr shows a typical section of rising main (Goldney's pitt barrells) but with a square clack door cast in. The author believes that in 1751 Coalbrookdale's technology was not sufficiently advanced to cast these apertures in the pipes and hence Arthers' men were chipping the holes in the cast iron instead. A laborious and delicate process.

The lowest of the pit barrels would have been positioned at the deepest point in the sump of the shaft and at its lower end had an enlarged section with a number of holes. These were to filter out the larger items of debris in the pit water that might block or damage the working of the pumps. The were produced in both parallel and egg ended versions and known as 'wind bore' or 'snore' on account of the noise they made when sucking a mix of air and water. The egg ended one illustrated is located beside the Elsecar engine house.

3.9 Willets & Wilding's Bill for Boiler Plates
(Nottingham University Ref Mi Av 168/35)

Mr Jarratt Smith ....Dr
To Willets & Wilding Framilode

1750	c q l			£ s d
Januy 9	11-0-11	Boiler Plates	@ 25s	13. 17. 7
15	7-1- 2	Boiler Plates	@ 25s	9. 1. 5
26	8-1-12	Boiler Plates	@ 25s	10. 9. 0
Febry 8	7-1-12	Boiler Plates	@ 25s	9. 4. 0
15	7-2- 0	Boiler Plates	@ 25s	9. 7. 6
21	6-1-18	Boiler Plates	@ 25s	8. 0. 3
		Freight of qt 2d parcell to Bristol		0. 1. 0
				£60. 0. 9

Commentary on Willets & Wilding's Bill

John Willets was one of the predecessors of the well known Spear and Jackson company and made a very successful business of producing edge tools and guns at his Wednesbury Forge for most of the 18th century.[28] Not much else is known of his company's boiler plate production but it would appear that the basic plates were produced by Willets at Wednesbury and taken down the Severn to Wilding's work at Framilode for further processing or simply for stock.

Willets, like Malcott the brass merchant also supplied boiler plates to John Wise for the first Chelsea waterworks engine in 1742[29] and subsequently supplied a whole boiler for the second engine in 1744[30] so appears to have had an established position and presumably a good reputation in this market.

George Wilding, (who died on 13th October 1766), was 'Master of iron mills at Framilode'[31] which, given its position near to the River Severn, was ideally located to take advantage of the water borne traffic up and down the river. Boiler plates may have been cut to size at Framilode which is known to have operated a slitting mill.[32] Replacement boiler plates were a frequent requirement and one assumes that they were ordered in bulk and fitted locally as required. It is interesting to note that the cost of these wrought iron plates at 25 shillings per cwt was nearly as much as for a bored cylinder, indicating the amount of smithing work needed to produce them.

Early boilers required frequent replacement of plates and Goldney's account book shows regular consignments of them

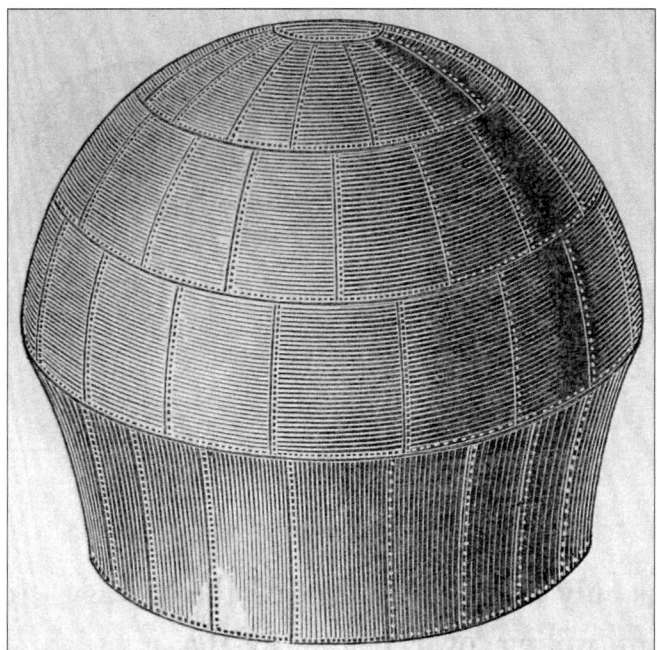

This image from the 1860s of a typical haystack boiler gives some idea of the shapes and numbers of the boiler plates as well as the number of rivet holed that would need to be punched.

to Jarrit Smith (for the LoW and possibly on his own account) and other Bristol Colliery owners. These may have come from Coalbrookdale or Goldney may simply have been acting as agent for other boiler plate makers.

3.10 Thomas Hills's Bill for Lead
(Nottingham University Ref MI Av 168/37)

Mesrs Jarrett Smith and Co; Owners
of the Fire Engine at Colepit Heath

1750					To Thomas Hills		
		c	q	l	£	s	d
Janry 24	To a Lead boyler top	32	1	7	at 16 C	25.17.	0
	To Lead pipes	20	1	25	at 21 C	21. 9.11	
	To a ring coller	1	0	2	at 2d L	19.	0
	To Sheet Lead for Cistern [___] Dash Cap [do]	29	1	23	at 14 C	20.12.	4
	To barr lead	2	3	22	at 12/9 C	1.17.	6¾
	To Soder	2	2	7		9. 0.	6½
	To work 11 days ¾ for 2 men					4. 2.	3
1751 April 9	To a Lead pipe	1	0	10		1. 2.10½	
	To Soder 18 £ ¾	0	11	8			
	To weights for the [Sestill]	1	1	23	at 2 D	1. 7.	2
	To barr lead	1	0	8		0.13.	7
	To work one Day for 2 men					0. 7.	0
						88. 0.11¼	

Commentary on Hills's Bill

Thomas Hills is described in other bills for the LoW[33] as a 'plumber', which the author takes to mean that he was a lead merchant and presumably a local one. His main bills for the

engine were for the lead and solder needed for the boiler and related steam and water pipework. Hills supplies over 4 tons of lead and prices range from 12s per cwt for barr lead to lead pipes at 21s per cwt. The latter presumably reflecting the work needed to both roll and form the lead into pipes. Hill's billing coincides with Goldney's and Arthers', in the busy period from January-April 1751. The small size of the second part of Hills bill from April 9th onwards suggests that his materials and men are being used for the final fitting out.

The most expensive item was the boiler top, all 32cwt of it. The reason for using a different material for the boiler top is not well documented, copper had also been used for tops (as well as whole boilers) and the use of both continued for some time after this. Lead was an easier material to work when it came to installing all the lead pipework at the top of the boiler and a single large lead-iron flange was easier to make and less likely to leak than the multiple lead-iron flanges needed if the boiler top was iron. The lead-iron combination set up an unfavourable electrolytic reaction that accelerated boiler corrosion. By the later part of the 18th century iron working had developed to the point that boilers could be made completely in iron.

It is noteworthy too that the last entry on Palmer's sundries bill is 'for loading the boiler top'. Given its weight of 32 cwt and the low tensile strength of lead, the arrangements for this must have presented some challenges.

The purpose of the 'ring coller' weighing around a hundredweight eludes the writer (possibly for the joint between boiler and top?). The 'cistern in the dash' is likely to be the water cistern at the top of the engine house.[34] At this time, so it is believed, it was cheaper and easier to make a cistern from lead rather than iron. What is also clear is that Hills has provided a team of specialists to do the following:

- Building and fitting the lead 'boyler top' onto the main body of the boiler.
- Adjusting, fitting and soldering all the pipework.
- Cutting, melting or rolling 'barr and sheet lead' into the required forms to make the boiler, water and steam pipes and ensure they did not leak.

3.11 William Tily's Bill for Timber
(Nottingham University Ref MI Av 168/38)

June ye 6 Jarrit Smith Esq and Comy. To Wm Tily [___ ___]
1751 [___] of the Fire Engine

	£	s	d
To 54 feet of 4 Inch Elm plank at 8d foot	1.	16.	0
To 63 feet of Inch and ½ plank ditto at 4 foot	1.	1.	0
To Charges in Halling of the said stuff [down]	0.	3.	0
	3.	**0.**	**0**

Commentary on Tily's Bill

The one and a half inch planks would almost certainly be for floor boarding on the two upper levels of the engine house. The purpose of the four inch thick elm boards are less obvious, these were substantial timbers and it is suggested that they were either used for the floor of the ground level where weights and loads would be substantially higher or for landings or other fittings in the shaft where elms tolerance for water was needed.

3.12 Ponsford's Bill for Leather
(Nottingham University Ref Mi Av 171/8)

Mr Jerrard Smith

1751   Bought of Wm Ponsford

1751 8 April	£	s	d
To ½ Bend 39 lb at 12d pr lb	1.	19.	0
To 2- 0-14 Cank Leather at 19d pr lb	7.	10.	5
	9.	9.	5

Commentary on Ponsford's Bill

It has not been possible to trace Mr Ponsford. Leather was widely used for a variety of purposes and it is expected that the LoW would have a choice of suppliers. The leather would probably have been used to make the clacks water tight and for the seal around the piston. The timing of the bill in early April fits with this. Note also that Palmer's sundries bill has an entry '*April 12 Paid Messrs Pidding for Leather Straps*'.

3.13 Hillhouse Getley and Co's Bill
(Nottingham University Ref Mi Av 194/3)

Jarrit Smith Esqr & Co

         To Hilhouse Getley & Co

1752		c w l				£ s d
20 April	To 17 Barrs Iron	3-2- 9	@18s 6d			3. 6. 3
July 19th	To 1 Cylonder	7-2-16	@20s	7.12.11		
	1 Frame	1-1-23	@14s	1. 0. 4		
	1 Clack seat	-1- 8	@18s 8d	0. 6. 0		
	Boring the above Cylinder		@10s	3.16. 6		
	Scouring the Clack Seat			0. 2. 6		
						12.18. 3
Decr 27	To 16 Barrs of Iron	4-2- 1	@18s 6d	4. 5. 5		
	1 Bundle Bst Fontrs Rods	-2- 0	@27s	13. 6	4.18.11	
1753						
Augt 23	To 4 Clacks	1-0-16	@28s		1.12. 0	
Octor 22	To 1 Brass Shiver	-1-14½	@12d	2. 2. 6		
	13 Brasses	-1-16½	do	2. 4. 6		
30	To 2 Small Cylonders	4-2- 0	20s	4.10. 0		
					8.17. 0	
1754						
Jany 5	To 1 Sheet single plate	-1- 8	@34s	0.10.10		
9	To 1 Cylonder Board	14-0-21	30s	21. 5. 8		
					21:16: 6	
Marh 2	To 4 Bucketts	1: 0:19	@23s 4d		1: 7: 4	
Aprl 1	To 2 Cylonders	4:0:25	@20s		4: 4: 6	
July 19	To 1 Door Frame	1:1: 5	@14s	0:18: 0		
20	To 1 Barr Iron	0:2:10	@18s	0:10: 8	1: 8: 8	

1755		c w l				£ s d
Decr 2	To 9 Barrs Sparr Iron	2-0-15	@19s			2. 0. 7
16	To 2 Barrs Iron Shutting ditto	2-2-26	@18s 6d	2.10. 7		
				. 2. 0		
						2.12. 7
1756						
July 14	To 1 Cylonder	1-0- 2	@20s			1. 0. 4
						66. 2.11
		Cr				
1754						
1 Aprl	By 1 Old Cylonder &c	5 cwt	@5s	1. 5. 0		
19 July	By 1 Old Frame	1:1:15	@4s	. 5. 6		
						1.10. 6
					Ball	64.12. 5

Commentary on Hillhouse Getley's Bill

This bill is particularly interesting as it covers the period after my assumed date for the commissioning of the engine (May 1751). It also involves Hillhouse billing in association with Getley (whose name appears with Hillhouse on Palmer's materials bill). The following points are of note:

- It starts very soon after Palmer's last bill on 20th April 1752 and continues for four years.
- It contains items that have been billed previously (such as bars of Iron, Clack, Shivers).
- On the 9th January 1754 a '*cylinder board*' weighing 14 cwt is billed for. I believe this would have been to replace the '*cylinder bottom*' supplied by Goldney (which was only slightly heavier at 15cwt). It would have been a major failure if this broke, requiring rebuilding of the engine (see following section).
- The other '*cylinders*' referred to are probably the buckets on the pump rods and as there is also work on '*clack seat, frames and doors*' it may have been that the pumps were causing trouble, a frequent occurrence by virtue of pit water containing sand and/or corrosion inducing chemicals.
- They give credit for an '*old cylinder*' and an '*old frame*'.
- Its timing cross references well with Nathaniel Arthers' second bill.

There are two distinct phases of bills, the first ending in December 1753 is only for minor items and apart from '*boring the above cylinder and scouring the clack seat*' includes no obvious entries for labour. The second phase of bills from January 1754 onwards is for more substantial items, namely repair of the engine and pitwork.

The most likely interpretation for the second phase of bills is that the engine was not working properly and the LoW commissioned Hillhouse Getley (and Arthers) to rectify or repair the work for which Palmer had previously overseen.

In this case it appears that Hillhouse and Getley are supplying more finished items as well as apparently charging for work done by their staff. See also section 3.4.2 on Hillhouse Getley.

Note that this bill does not state that it is for the 'Fire Engine', this is a deduction on the part of the author.

3.14 Nathaniel Arthers's (second) Bill for Smithing and Metal Work (BRO Ref AC/AS 97/3)

Jarrett Smith & Co

To Nathaniel Arthur Dr

1752		£ s d
June 19	To 1 Joint Rod 2 ft [__] of Straps Square with Eye to Do flap Rod wt 2: 0: 2 @ 6d /lb	5.13. 0
Nov 27	To 2 ft of Plates & 12 Screw bolts to Do for buckets wt 27½ @ 6d	0.13. 9
Dec 12	To 3 Long Screw Bolts wt 13 @ 6	0. 6. 6
22	To 20 Bolts & Nuts 0: 2: 17 @ 6d	1.16. 6
1754		
Jan 5	To a New Regalter 13 @ 6d	0. 6. 6
30	To 4 Large Screw bolts 2 ft [__] of Plates 2 Dagers & 2 Clacks 0: 2: 19 @ 6	1:17: 6
	To 4 Sweep Bars for ye Pistern 0: 2: 24 3½d	1: 3: 4
March 2	To 2 Joints 2 Dagers & keys 0: 1: 10¼ @ 6d	0:19: 1½
11	To 1½ Inch Tap	0: 2: 0
30	To 20 + headed pins & 20 Do Square @ 3d	0:10: 0
April 2	To Laying ye Joints with Mending Do & New holes & [ading] Iron to Do	1: 0: 0
	To 20 Screw bolts 4 Inches Long 22½ @ 6d	0:11: 3
	To Screw plate & 3 Taps	1: 1: 0
17	To Mending a Vice with a New box to Do & 3 New Washers & Cuting ye Chops	0:19: 0
May 17	To 41 Square headed pins @ 3d per pin	0:10: 3
	To 36 + headed pins @ 3d per pin	0: 9: 0
	To 347 pins Screws & Nuts to Do @ 3d	4: 6: 9
		22: 5: 5½
1754	Continued & Brote Over	**£ s d**
May 7	To the Total Sum Brote Over	**22: 5: 5½**
	To 30 Larger Sort of pins 16½ @ 6d	0: 8: 3
July 19	To hooks & hinges for ye Boiler Door wt 17½ @ 6	0: 8: 9
	To 3 Men making ye Boiler Bottom	5:10: 0
	To Rivet for Do wt 0: 2: 24¼ @ 5d	1:13: 5¼
Nov 18	To New Joints & fitting 2 Dagers to Each Joint wt 0: 1: 18 @ 6d	1: 3: 0
	To Mending a Chain with 3 New Links & Cuting & Shuting ye hooks wt 0: 1: 2½ @ 6	0:15: 3
		32: 4: 1¾
	By old Iron Recd 3 Links 2 Joints 0: 1: 7 @ 1½	0: 4: 4½
		31:19: 9¼

Commentary on Arthers' (second) Bill

When the contents and dates of Arthers' bill are looked at in conjunction with those of Hillhouse Getley, some patterns are evident. Arthers' bills during 1752 of just over £8 are mostly for small items of ironwork that would be needed for running repairs and/or pitwork, there are none in 1753. The bills in 1754, however, are for larger and more complex items, starting off with a new *regalater* (albeit at a fraction of the cost of Malcott's regulator) and '*4 sweep bars for ye pistern*' which are thought to be new mountings for the piston stem on its plate which presumably were secured by the '*4 large screw bolts*'. This does appear to fit with the entry in Arthurs' first bill for drilling and cutting four new holes in the piston.

When Hillhouse's bill for a '*new cylinder board*' and the coincidence of the billing date of January 1754 are also taken into account, the author suggests the most likely explanation is that the piston had 'overstroked', making contact with the cylinder bottom, damaging the cylinder base and breaking the bearing connecting the piston and stem. This damage would have occurred late in December 1754 and it does not stretch credibility too far to imagine there may have been a seasonal influence here.

Throughout the history of the beam engine there are instances of damage to engines caused by 'overstroking' when the piston exceeds its normal stroke to the extent that it strikes and damages the cylinder base (or in the case of later engines with enclosed cylinders, the cylinder cover). The most common cause of this was a sudden breakage in the pitwork, which would make the outdoor beam end rise suddenly (as it was now out of balance) past its normal limit of travel. The corresponding descent of the indoor beam end would cause the piston to strike the cylinder base. The damage caused would depend on the force of the impact, with the most extreme being a shattered piston and cylinder. In this case it appears that the impact did not break the cylinder but damaged the supporting cylinder base such that it needed replacing and breaking the primitive crosshead between piston plate and stem.

This would have stopped the engine with the result that the coal workings below the water table may have become flooded and this would remain the case for some time after the engine restarted.

It also appears that in July 1755, the boiler was rebuilt as Arthers charges for '*making ye boiler bottom* and *to hooks and hinges for ye boiler doors*'. Hillhouse bills for a '*Door Frame*' on 19th July which is interpreted as a new frame for the boiler doors. It has been suggested that pins are another term for bolt[35] even though the term bolt is used in the same document.

3.15 Geo Wildings Bill for Boiler Plates (BRO Ref AC/AS 93 section 15)

Jarrett Smith Esq   [___] Dr To Geo Wilding

1755		c q l			£	s	d
Aug 30th	To	1-1- 26	Plates	@ 27s	2.	0.	0
Sept 8th	To	12-1- 3	Plates	@ 27s	16.	11.	6
					£18.	**11.**	**6**

Commentary on Wilding's Bill

No comment other than the absence of Willets.

CHAPTER 3 References

1. R. A. Mott., *Abraham Darby (I and II) and the Coal Iron Industry* Transactions of the Newcomen Society 1957 pp 49-93.

2. Torsten and Peter Berg, *R R Angerstein's Illustrated Travel Diary 1753-1755 Industry In England and Wales from a Swedish Perspective* (Science Museum 2001) ISBN 1900747243,p 333

3. C. Evans and G. Ryden G., *Baltic Iron in the atlantic world in the eighteenth century* (Brill 2007), ISBN 97889004161535.

4. Angerstein p128.

5. J. Penny, *Bristol at Work* (Bredon Books 2005) ISBN 1859833551, pp143-148.

6. Getley's will of March 1784 is held in the BRO under reference 11982/18.

7. Pers' comm', Peter King.

8. Angerstein, pp 258/9.

9. Angerstein, pp 267/8.

10. Angerstein, p 140.

11. Pers' comm David Cranstone.

12. Baltic Iron.

13. Baltic Iron.

14. Pers' comm', David Cranstone.

15. The Elton family have a long connection with Bristol, being involved in a wide range of industries and were also connected with Abraham Darby. The Elton referred to here would be the third Baron 1703-1761.

16. D. B. Barton, *The Cornish Beam Engine* (D. Bradford Barton 1969) ISBN 187106004.

17. LMA, Acc.2558/CH/1/9 Chelsea Water Works, Court of Directors Minute Book No. 10 (Sept 1739-Mar 1743) Payment to James Malcott on June 3rd 1742.

18. BRO F/Bond/5/7 of 22/9/1759.

19. BRO FCW/1761/5.

20. Examination of way that the joints between the components of the Iron Bridge over the River Severn at Ironbridge makes it clear that in the early days of cast iron construction the principles of carpentry were used – there were after all no recognised alternatives. The framing of the 1845 Neath Abbey beam winding engine at Glyn Pits, shows how long this practice survived – see Marylyn Palmer and Peter Neaverson, *The Steam Engines at Glyn Pits Colliery – an archaeological investigation* Industrial Archaeology Review Vol X111 Number 1 Autumn 1990,pp 7-34.

21. K. Rogers, p12.

22. P. K. Stembridge, *The Goldney Family – A Bristol Merchant Dynasty* (Bristol Record Publications No. 54 1998) ISSN 0901538191.

23. A. Raistrick, *Dynasty of Ironfounders* (Ironbridge Gorge Museums Trust, reprinted 1989) ISBN 185072 0584.

24. *Ibid.*

25. WRO 473/295.

26. *Ibid.*

27. C. Green, *Severn Traders* (Black Dwarf 1999) ISBN 0953302822, pp 143/144.

28. Belford, P., *Five centuries of iron working: excavations at Wednesbury Forge.* (Post-Medieval Archaeology 44/1 (2010) pp 1-53).

29. LMA, Acc.2558/CH/1/9 Chelsea Water Works, Court of Directors Minute Book No. 10 (Sept 1939-Mar 1743) pp. 152-158.

30. LMA Acc.2558/CH/1/9 Chelsea Water Works, Court of Directors Minute Book No. 11 (April 1743-Feb 1748) pp 181/2 and 215.

31. A. Chatwin, Some Gloucestershire Ironmasters, *Journal of the Historical Metallurgy Society* Vol. 31 No. 1 1997 p 22.

32. *Ibid.*

33. Nottingham University Mi Av 179 1-69 in which Hills charges for solder for the 'great house'.

34. Peter Tymkow has advised the author that 'dach' is an old German term for roof and dash may therefore be a derivative. The cistern would be the cold water reservoir, located as high as possible in the engine house to maximise the pressure of the water used for injection into the cylinder to condensed the steam.

35. Pers Comm, Geoff Hayes

Opposite: Anderson's image of the Pentrich cylinder mouth was taken with the piston toward the bottom of its stroke. It appears that a series of heavy metal objects (some of which appear to be firebars) were tied to the chains presumably to balance the beam. This suggests that material had been added to the pitwork. It looks untidy but it was probably effective.

Reproduced by courtesy of the Science Museum/Science & Society Picture Library

No apologies for using another of Mr Anderson's superb images of the Pentrich Engine. This one shows the indoor section of the beam and the cistern for the water feed.
Reproduced by courtesy of the Science Museum/Science & Society Picture Library

Chapter 4
INSIGHTS and CONCLUSIONS

The total costs of the engine, when the second phase of work is take into account, amount to £975 19s 9½d, (see Section 1.8) to which needs to be added the £259 which has been interpreted as an internal charge from the estate (see Section 2.6) giving a total of £1,234 19s 9½d.

An investment of this magnitude in 1751 was a significant one, equal to approximately £181,000[1] at 2003 values and particularly noteworthy as the LoW partnership was relatively new. It is assumed that Middleton's experience with previous Newcomen installations in Nottinghamshire combined with Jarrit's intimate knowledge of the nature of the local coal measures gave the partners the confidence to make a commitment of this nature.

Overall this confidence would appear to have been justified, even allowing that my assumptions about the problems with the engine are valid, as by the 1780s and probably earlier the LoW's colliery operations were making profits in the order of around a third of total revenue.[2]

Although there were other local pits, Coalpit Heath coal appears to have enjoyed a good reputation for quality,[3] accounts from the 1780s[4] indicating it was transported as far as Chippenham and Dursley, distances of twenty or so miles over roads as yet unimproved by turnpike trusts.

4.2 The Context of the LoW Accounts

The reason for maintaining such comprehensive accounts appears to have been to allow full financial transparency between the three partners in LoW. Given Jarrit's background in law, Middleton's experience with mining operations and Colston's extensive commercial background, it is natural that they would require full accounts to be maintained.

The history of the Smythes of Ashton Court and Jarrit Smith's acquisition of their estate is set out in detail in Anton Bantocks account of the family[5] and only a brief outline, relevant to his mining activities is given here. Jarrit's father John Smith lived at Mayshill at the northern end of the coalfield and was clerk to the Berkeley family when they held that part of the Manor of Westerleigh in the later 17th Century. Jarrit was a successful Bristol lawyer and this is understood to have been the basis of his initial wealth. He acquired his portion of the Manor of Westerleigh in 1741 in settlement of debts resulting from the bankruptcy of the incumbent, Sir John Smyth II to whom Jarrit had already made substantial loans. Jarrit also married Florence the daughter of John Smythe 1 (note that although Jarrit's descendants adopted the Smythe spelling – Jarrit Smith was not related by blood to the Smythe family).

Mayshill farmhouse, understood to have been built by Jarrit Smith and used as his local residence

Like his father, Jarrit was involved in coal mining around Mayshill and after the LoW partnership was formalised in 1746, continued to operate pits in the area on his own account[6]. He also acquired the mineral rights to land south of the River Avon in Bristol around Bedminster and made substantial investments to develop the section of coalfield he controlled.[7]

Jarrit had a number of homes and Mayshill farm built by him around 1740, appears to have been his local one and still stands today, largely in its original form.

4.3 How Long did the Round Engine House Survive?

The documentary evidence does confirm that the engine house was round. The case for the round engine house being the 1751 Engine is as follows:

- The LoW are understood to have commissioned a total of four Newcomen Engines between 1751 and 1791. The author is confident of his attribution of the 1791 Serridge Engine to its location at ST 675796 based on the ongoing SGMRG excavations at the site[8]. The author is similarly confident of the location of Ram Engine at ST675803 on the basis of the evidence of multiple maps[9] and the remaining open shaft top.

- This leaves the two earlier engine houses drawn by Sturge in 1786 from Hall's 1772 survey[10] one of rectangular form at ST672802 and the round one about 300 yards to the North East at ST676803.

- When the LoW commissioned the Serridge Engine, their contract of 1789[11] required Messrs Palmer and Bond to keep in repair the other two engines, confirming that one of the previous three was no longer in use.

- The letter from Tho's Humphries and Dan'l James of 16th May 1792 tells us that '*if the assistance of more engines than we at present have should be found necessary, it is intended to affix an additional cylinder to that engine which now stands on that part of the common called Ramhill* (the Ram Engine) *which cylinder together with several of its necessary appendages is now lodged in the old round engine house*'[12].So by 1792 it appears that the 1751 Engine was not in use as such and the author can find no references to it in any subsequent materials. (This latter entry is particularly intriguing, suggesting that compounding of Newcomen engines was a recognised option at this time, Jonathan Hornblower having erected the first one at Radstock is 1782[13]).

- The local parish map drawn up in 1845, a version of which is held by BRO under ref AC/PL/124_2, shows what appears to be the LoWs surface land holdings marked in blue. This map shows the access road to the rectangular engine house and the area around the engine clearly marked (*opposite*). There are no markings or features of any nature denoting the location of the Round Engine House. On this basis it is concluded that the site reverted had reverted to agricultural purposes by this time and the engine house would have been dismantled to enable the reuse of the materials sometime after 1792.

- The Coal Authority hold a most interesting map (Ref R333) that names (amongst other features) only Ram, Serridge and Old Engine (i.e. the rectangular engine house). This map is thought to be the only full record of an early self-contained internal railway system, the function of which appears to have been to supply the pumping pits with the large quantities of the coal needed for their boilers from the coal raising pits.

The second Newcomen engine at Coalpit Heath which the author believes was constructed around 1763 and which appears on nineteenth century maps under the title 'Old Engine', suggesting it was the oldest then in use locally. The left-hand image is from Halls 1772 survey delineated by Sturge in 1786 (BRO AC/PL89-1). The image on the right shows 'Old Engine' again, this time from BRO AC/PL 89-2, apparently in the hand of a different artist.

Both reproduced by courtesy of the BRO

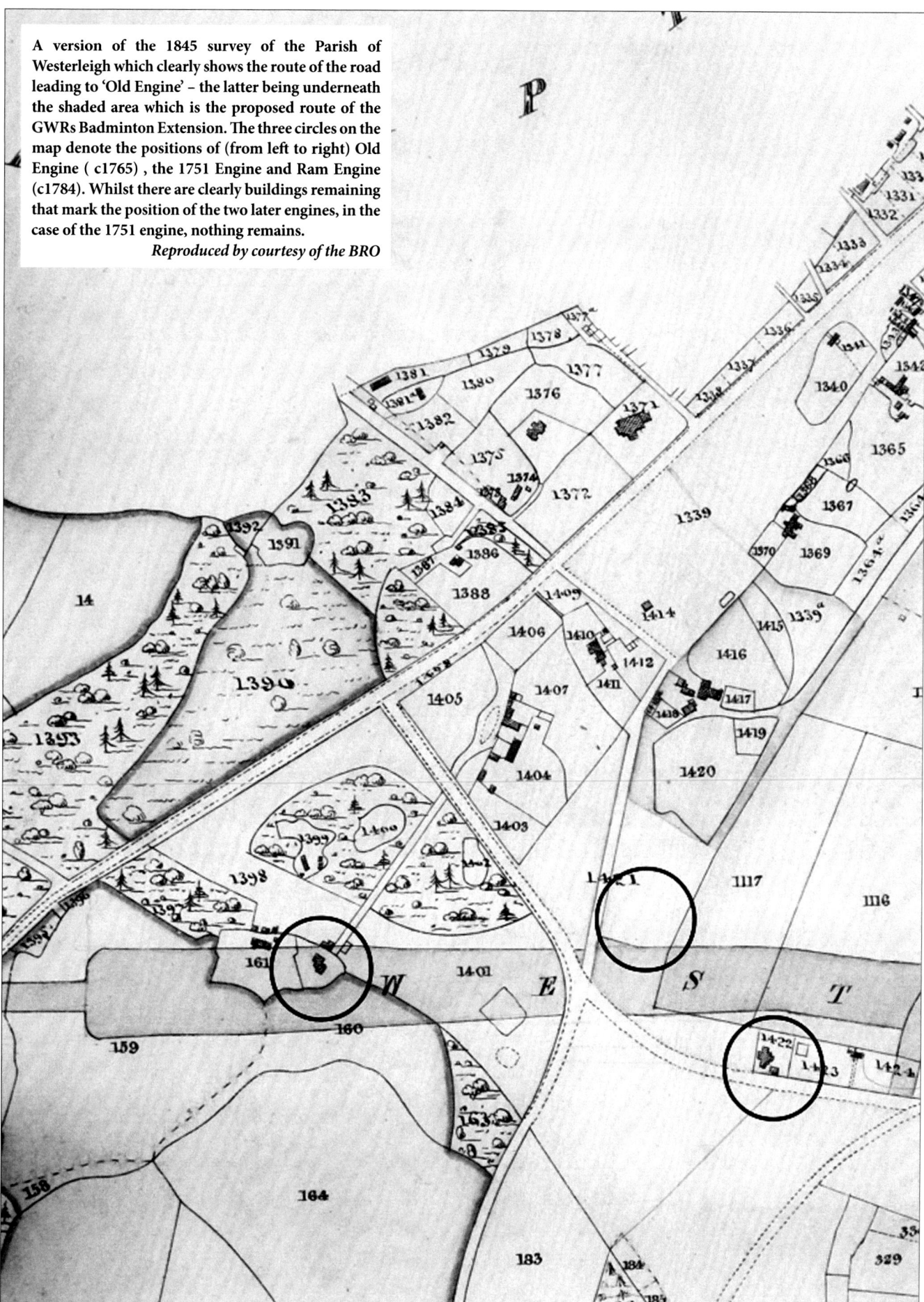

A version of the 1845 survey of the Parish of Westerleigh which clearly shows the route of the road leading to 'Old Engine' – the latter being underneath the shaded area which is the proposed route of the GWRs Badminton Extension. The three circles on the map denote the positions of (from left to right) Old Engine (c1765) , the 1751 Engine and Ram Engine (c1784). Whilst there are clearly buildings remaining that mark the position of the two later engines, in the case of the 1751 engine, nothing remains.

Reproduced by courtesy of the BRO

The 1751 engine site is not marked on this map, suggesting it was not longer in use. This map, whilst undated is understood to have been drawn up around 1800.

- The main thrust of any counter argument in favour of 'Old Engine' being the 1751 engine is limited to its name on the above map and its location at what is thought to be a shallower point on the coal seams.

4.4 The Arguments for Internal or External Boilers

Newcomen Engines were initially built with their boilers below the cylinder within the confines of the engine house. This imposed the following limitations on their strength and maintainability:

- The size of the boiler and therefore its steam raising capacity (and so the power of the engine) was limited by the dimensions of the engine house.
- As the cylinder was mounted above the boiler on heavy timber baulks set into the engine house walls, increasing the boiler and therefore the engine house size would reduce the strength of this already less than ideal arrangement (and increase building costs).

An internal view of the 1712 replica engine installed at the Black Country Museum. It gives a good view of the general layout of early engines, note the cylinder mounted on the massive oak beams.

- Repair and replacement of the boiler, its plates or other features would need to be undertaken within the cramped confines of the engine house. There are two remaining Newcomen engine houses locally with large arches built into the basement walls, presumably to facilitate access for work on the boiler.

Between 1762 and 1765 five very large engines with Coalbrookdale supplied cylinders of between 60- and 75-inches were commissioned on Tyneside, to drain the deep and rich coal seams upon which the area had made its reputation. To provide a contingency in case of boiler failure (which would quickly lead to the workings flooding in these deep and wet mines) a number of these installations had two or more boilers. Gabriel Jars, a Frenchman, reporting the first one, a 74-inch engine installed in 1762 at Walker Colliery having a total of four boilers.[14]

By definition, these boilers were located outside the engine house, the only disadvantage apparently being a longer run of pipework for the steam. This arrangement appears to have been successful as these engines operated for some time until replaced by later Boulton and Watt ones. The reason for this diversion is to highlight that by 1762 the use of external boilers on Newcomen installations was an established practice and it is possible that Palmer was aware of this in 1751 and constructed his engine accordingly.

There is a widely accepted view that the use of external boilers dates from the 1790s but the evidence for this appears to centre around the publication of Currs guide at this time, Rolt and Allen[15] attributing the initial instances of this practice to this period[15]. Whilst the evidence is extremely thin (pictorial only) the author wonders if Palmer and the LoW had anticipated Curr by forty years? The author also suspects that other engine builders had recognised the advantages of external boilers prior to 1790.

It is however possible that what the author has interpreted as an external boiler on the 1751 map is in fact a second boiler and the primary boiler is within the house in the normal location.

4.5 Building and Maintaining Early Boilers

These days we take for granted the advances in materials technology that have taken place since the 18th century and can therefore easily underestimate the challenges facing the engineers that built and maintained early boilers. The following points may help the reader appreciate these difficulties better.

4.5.1 Construction

Boilers were built up from half inch thick wrought iron plates that had been cut to standard sizes, the first challenge was to form them into the haystack shape of a boiler. Handling these plates was a difficult task because of their weight and size and the author believes that Arthers' forge would have been equipped with a small hand crane or a similar device for lifting and positioning the plates. Forming the curves on the plates would have been a hard and laborious process and the smiths may have been assisted by some arrangement for mechanising the hammer.

For a number of years and certainly after 1751, boilers were built with a separate copper or lead domes or tops. This is presumed to be because the challenges of incorporating multiple pipework and junctions into a dome built up of wrought iron plates was beyond the ironworking skills of the time.

The seams joining the plates were secured by rivets (which Curr gives the ideal dimensions as being half an inch diameter) and these needed additional sealing as metal to metal joints leaked. The materials used for sealing are not obvious from the bills, solder would suffice on some areas away from the fire but was too expensive for widespread use and it is probable that Oakum or a similar form of fibrous seal would have been used.

Engineering work that we take for granted these days such as producing matched sets of rivet holes in adjacent plates would have needed considerable skill in 1751. A challenging exercise in three dimensional metal working with a minimum of mechanical aids in a dimly lit temporary smithy in the depths of winter. It would be an interesting exercise to recreate this process.

The Science Museums cutaway model of a haystack boiler, its settings and ancillaries helps understand some of the challenges involved with constructing and maintaining such boilers.

4.5.2 Operation and Maintenance

Filling the boiler with water increases the load on both boiler and mountings and would produce additional stresses. The slow corrosive action of water on iron over time would be accelerated if impure water was used and this was often a cause for concern in early boilers

The application of heat to the boiler base and sides (via the spiral flue built into the firebrick surround of the boiler sides) caused damage and wear from the regular expansion and contraction. The heat also accelerated corrosion around any weaknesses, imperfections or scale accumulations in the wrought iron plates.

Boiler plates would need regular repair and sometimes complete replacement and Goldney's account book shows a steady stream of orders for replacement plates to both Jarrit Smith and other customers.

Boiler plate replacement entailed challenges additional to those described above. If done in situ, removal of sufficient masonry to access the boiler was required and built up scale from the boiler interior would need to be chipped off before repair starts. If the size of the task was such that the boiler would need replacement this could presumably only be undertaken by dismantling the boiler and then reversing the process to rebuild it. An external boiler would at least have been easier to access.

Continuity of operation was obviously important and it appears to have become general practice to have a spare boiler at hand. Where this was not available, no pumping could be done whilst the fires were drawn, the boiler cooled, the repairs were done and the boiler returned to working temperature after repair. It is a great pity we have no accounts of this unglamorous but crucial role.

4.6 Blacksmiths – a Forgotten Skill

Because iron casting and moulding technology was still in its infancy and only simple shapes could be produced, all ironwork for the engine linkages, valve gear and controls, fixings, straps, nuts, braces etc. were blacksmith made. It was the blacksmiths task to make all the components so that the engine not only worked, but was robust enough to continue doing so.

Close examination of the smaller components of the few remaining 18th century Newcomen engines show that most were fashioned with considerable skill in terms of their shape and also the distribution of weight within them.

This image of the Pentrich engine controls shows the graceful and slightly irregular features of blacksmith made components.

This image of the cylinder base fixings on the Pentirch engine show how the resourceful blacksmiths managed to produce effective fixings.

Producing a bespoke piece of ironwork by hand and eye to a precise size is difficult enough even for a skilled blacksmith. In addition they had to be capable of tempering and annealing the iron and steel to meet the demands of its application as a matter of routine. The skills of such men have been held in high regard since the early days of smithing. Much attention has been given to the 'lives of the engineers' but very little to the skilled artisans who provided the expertise to bring their inventions to fruition. The growth of large scale ironworking from the 19th century onwards did not at first displace these men, their skills were adapted to the larger scale operations and their application on an industrial scale could still be recognised until well into the 20th century.

In this country outside of the farriers trade, the blacksmiths skill has been almost completely lost and because of this it is difficult for us to appreciate how important it was. This is an entirely separate area of study and the author's purpose here is to highlight the importance of the smith's role. For an overview of the Blacksmiths skills Dorothy Hartley's book – *Made in England* is recommended.[16]

4.7 Installations of Newcomen Engines around Bristol

There were concentrations of early Newcomen Engines in Cornwall's metal mines and the coalfields of Tyneside, the Black Country and Warwickshire. The Bristol coalfield was one of the areas that followed rapidly with a significant number of installations from the 1740s onwards.

SGMRG are planning to produce a full inventory of Newcomen installations in the Bristol region, building on the excellent foundation provided by Ken Rogers. However for the purposes of this account a brief overview is given below.

The earliest engines that we can identify with reasonable confidence are three engines at Kingswood, Hanham and Brislington built by John Wise of Hawkesbury between 1737 and 1740.[17] and there is every possibility that he built others locally after 1742. The source of the cylinders and other major components for these engines is unclear, Wise ordered the cylinder for the 1742[18] engine he built for Chelsea waterworks from William Bowen, a charcoal Iron founder in the Weald and the cylinders for his Bristol engines may have been sourced from there too.

Goldney's account book.[19] the basis of Ken Rogers work commences in 1742 and runs through to 1769 listing deliveries of engine castings to over twenty customers in and around Bristol. Most of these were to collieries north of the Avon but with a few to the south including the first to the Somerset Pits (Paulton in 1745). The largest and best known local installation was the 1761 engine with a 74½-inch cylinder at Warmley Brassworks, which was used to return water to power the water wheels which provided the blast for the furnaces.

Angerstein's 1754 sketch shows the Warmley Brassworks 48-inch engine that preceded the 1761 engine.

Image reproduced by courtesy of Peter Berg

Donnes Map of 1769 shows engines at Hanham, Kingswood, Pucklechurch, Nibley, Coalpit Heath and Yate and installations are recorded later at locations as diverse as Cromhall, Bitton and Two Mile Hill. Kanefsky and Roberts give the total of Newcomen engines in use in Gloucestershire by 1780 as 40, only the heavily industrialised Counties of Northumberland, Durham, W. Yorks, Shropshire and Cornwall exceeded this number.[20]

Whilst there were a number of Boulton and Watt engines installed for pumping from 1780 onwards, Newcomen engines continued to be built, relocated and used locally until the end of the 19th century. South Liberty Colliery at Ashton Vale was famous for continuing to use a Newcomen Engine from the 1760s in largely unaltered form until 1900.[21]

As Bristol's industrial base continued to grow throughout the 18th century it is probable some local companies were able to produce the major components such as cylinders and pipes.[22] Bristol's iron industry would have continued to develop to meet the needs of the local ship building industry and by the early 19th century companies such as Acraman appeared to have developed a good local business for engines and ironwork.

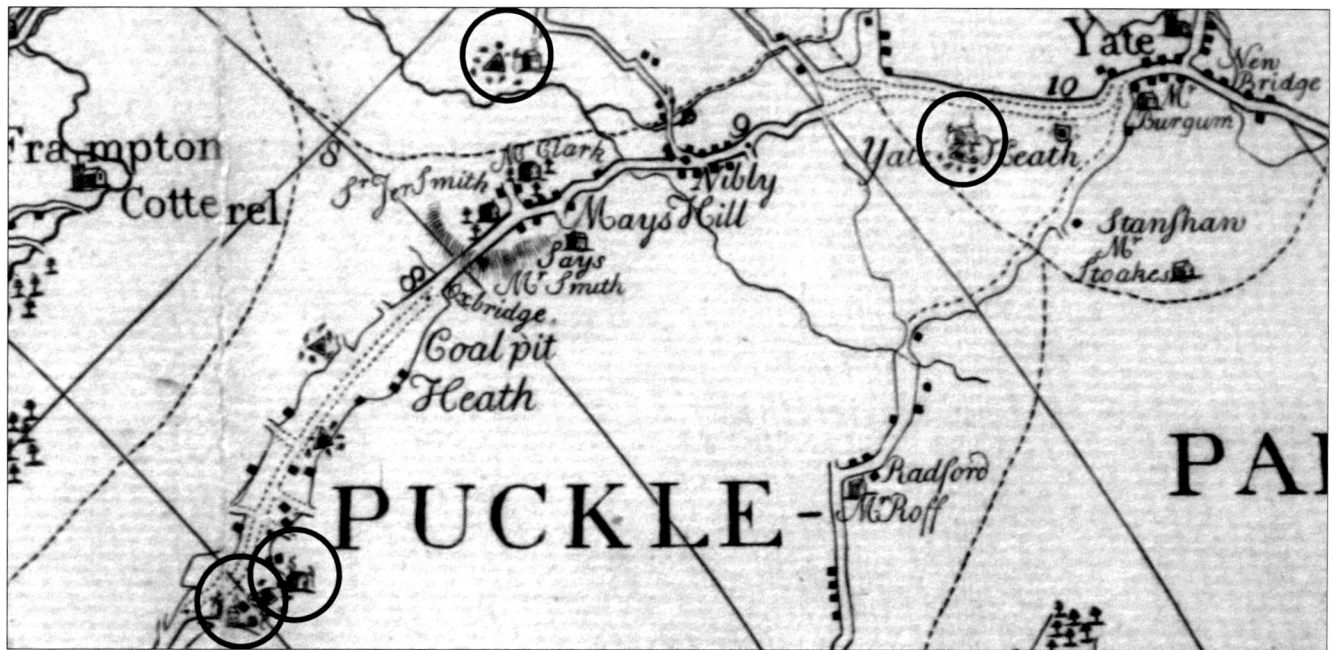

This extract from Donnes map of 1769 shows from circled (left to right) two engine houses at Coalpit Heath, one at Nibley and a fourth at Yate Heath about which nothing is known.

Courtesy Bristol Museums and Art Galleries

CHAPTER 4 References

1. J. O'Donaghue, *Consumer Price Inflation since 1750*, Economic Trends, No 604 ISSN 0013-0400.
2. The distribution of moneys between the LoW was carefully recorded and many of the documents in the BRO Ashton Court Papers in the AC/AS/97 series report this. It would appear that as a general rule, their established mining operations made profits in the order of 50% of revenues.
3. Notts Univ MiE 20/4/3 *thoughts of the two lines on halls plan* ND circa 1790, from an unnamed individual commenting on the relative merits of the two canal proposals surveyed by Hall (presumed to be the Hall responsible for the 1772 survey of Westerleigh). The letter refers to the inferior quality of the Cromhall Coal being best suited for lime burning, that of Rangeworthy being better *but that coal is yet inferior to Coalpit Heath: The superiority of Westerleigh coal being well known eastwards.*
4. BRO AC/AS 96- 1 and 2. Two large ledgers from the early 1780s listing the daily shipments from each pit and the name and location of every customer. Whilst most customers were local and to the north of Coalpit Heath in the Severn Vale, they also show that coal was routinely carried as far as Dursley and Chippenham, distances of 20 miles.
5. A. Bantock, *The Earlier Smythes of Ashton Court from their letters 1545-1741*, Malago Publications 1982 ISBN 0950781304.
6. The BRO's Ashton Court papers hold extensive materials relating to Jarrit and his fathers mining activities around Mayshill. They are too numerous to list in full but specific examples include:
   -AC/AS/93 -bill of 5th June 1754 from Thomas Deane to Jerard (sic) Smith for Pit Ropes at Mayshill.
   -AC/AS/97/5 –list of Mayshill Receipts and Payments.
7. The history of the Jarrits activities in Bedminster need to be properly researched. Matt Southway in Kingswood Coal Part 3 (reprinted by and available from SGMRG under ISBN 9780955346422) gives a good overview of this initiative. The earliest reference the author has located appears to be BRO 4168/23, a 1754 coaling lease from Ann Smythe to Jarrit Smith and others. The Smythe family's involvement in mining here ending in 1906 with the closure of Dean Lane Colliery.
8. SGMRG excavations at the 1791 Serridge engine site commenced in 2006 and are still (2012) ongoing.
9. BRO AC/PL/89_1 and 2, Coal Authority R333.
10. BROS AC/PL/89_1 and 2.
11. BRO AC/AS//97/9 -Agreement dated 12th June 1789 between Thomas Palmer and Robert Bond and the representatives of the LoW to construct the Serridge engine.
12. BRO AC/AS/97/12.
13. R. Jenkins, Joseph Hornblower and The Compound Engine TNS Vol 11 1935 pp138-155
14. Rogers, p49.
15. Rolt and Allen, p125.
16. D. Hartley, *Made in England* First Published in 1939 Eyre Methuen 1977 ISBN 413314502 pp 139-147.
17. LMA, Acc.2558/CH/1/9 Chelsea Water Works, Court of Directors Minute Book No 10 (Sept 1739-Mar 1743) pp152-158.
18. *Ibid.,* p178.
19. WRO 473/295.
20. Kanefsky J and Roberts J *Steam Engines in 18th Century Britain: A quantitative assessment.* Technology and Culture Vol 21 1980, p176.
21. *Engineering,* 25th October 1895
22. J. Cornwell *The Bristol Coalfield*, Landmark Publishing 2003, ISBN 1843060949, p181 refers to a windbore found near the site of Grimsbury Pit in the 1980s that was reported to have been made on 4/3/1777 by Messrs Jones and Company, 40 St. Phillips Plain Bristol. This item is on display (2012) at the Kingswood Museum, Warmley.

Appendix 1
SELECTED BIBLIOGRAPHY

1. Rogers, K., *The Newcomen Engine in the West of England,* (Moonraker Press 1976), ISBN 239001575.
Ken Rogers, whilst employed as Wiltshire Archivist, came across Thomas Goldney's account book and recognised it had escaped the attention of researchers into early Newcomen Engines and the Coalbrookdale Company. He researched the customers listed as receiving Fire Engine components and added further information relating to the area, publishing the result in 1976. It remains the single most useful reference source for early engines in the region.

2. Raistrick, A., *Dynasty of Ironfounders,* (Ironbridge Gorge Museums Trust, reprinted 1989), ISBN 1850720584.
The late Arthur Raistrick, having written extensively about such topics needs little introduction to Industrial Archaeology devotees. This book, first published in 1953 remains the standard work on the Darby family and the Coalbrookdale Company.

3. Rolt, L. T. C. & Allen, J. S. *The steam engine of Thomas Newcomen,* (Landmark Publishing 1997, ISBN 190152244.
The late Tom Rolt, like Raistrick, was one of the pioneers of Industrial Archaeology and produced a biography of Newcomen under the title *Thomas Newcomen. The Prehistory of the Steam Engine.* John Allen, himself an expert on Newcomen Engines enlarged and revised Rolt's work under the title above. It is the best single reference source on Newcomen Engines.

4. Curr, J., *The Coal Viewer and Engine Builders Practical Companion,* (Augustus M Kelley, Reprinted 1970), ISBN 678051046.
Curr, a successful Sheffield Colliery Manager published in 1797, this extremely detailed quantity surveyor's guide to constructing a Newcomen engine. The line drawings contained within this book have been used to illustrate some of the components of the 1751 engine.

5. Berg, Torsten and Peter R. R., *Angerstein's Illustrated Travel Diary 1753-1755 Industry In England and Wales from a Swedish Perspective,* (Science Museum 2001) ISBN 1900747243.
David Cranstone, Chair of the Historical Metallurgy Society provided extensive guidance and assistance relating to the Iron and Steel used on the 1751 engine and opened the door onto what was a previously unknown field for me. Angerstein's book was probably the most helpful of all the sources that David highlighted. In addition to providing much insight into the Bristol region it also contains some excellent sketches made by Angerstein during his travels around England and Wales.

6. Evans C. and Ryden G., *Baltic Iron in the atlantic world in the eighteenth century,* (Brill 2007), ISBN 97889004161535.
Another introduction from David Cranstone. This well researched study of the links between the production of Swedish Iron, its processing in the UK (with much focus on the role of Bristol) and the sale of finished Iron products in the African and American colonies gives an invaluable insight into one aspect of the UKs economic leadership.

7. Rosen W., *The most powerful idea in the world – a story of steam, industry and invention,* (Pimlico 2011), ISBN 9781845951351.
Perhaps my most inspiring book of all, a very easy to read study of how the combination of economic, social and political developments in the England enabled it to be the cradle of the industrial revolution.

Appendix 2
THE PALMER FAMILY, A SUMMARY OF REFERENCES

The preceding account makes clear it is hoped, the author's interest in Charles Palmer who as engine wright, appears to be the central figure in the construction of the 1751 engine. It is believed that the work of Palmer and his relatives is a subject worthy of further study and the purpose of this summary is to list the known references to the Palmer family as a basis for this.

Charles Palmer and Thomas Palmer appear on accounts of building, dismantling and valuing Newcomen Engines in the Bristol and South Gloucestershire area on a number of occasions in the second half of the 18th Century. Their address is generally given as Mangotsfield (i.e. the parish of) and occasionally Staple Hill.

The Terrier (AC/PL 58) that accompanies the 1781 Survey of Kingswood Common (AC/PL 90) lists Arthur Palmer as owning a windmill located on the summit of Lodge Hill, adjacent to Kingswood Lodge (residence of the Duke of Beaufort's Colliery Bailiff) with five active pits and two Newcomen engines nearby. Section 3.4 sets out the author's assertion that Engine Wrights of the time would have learned and developed their expertise on wind and water mills and Arthur Palmer, who is believed to be the father of Charles is therefore ideally placed for this.

The eighteenth century references to individuals with the Palmer surname on matters relating to Newcomen engines and/or coal mining that the author is aware of are as follows:

- The 1748 Duke of Beaufort's Lodge Hill Coalworks Weekly Accounts (GA Badminton Muniments D2700/QP12/3) suggests that their "Fire Engine" became operational around 8 August 1748. This is deduced from:
- The change of title from "Lodge Coal Works" to the "Fire Engine Coalworks",
- The cessation of payments to the "water halliers"

- The commencement of payment to the 'enginemen' two of whom went by the name of Palmer. On the basis of his higher pay, the author assumes Arthur Palmer to be the senior and John the junior, possibly father and son (but no relationship established with Charles Palmer)
- In 1760 - Charles Palmer provides an estimate for building a waterwheel to pump water from Thomas Haynes colliery at Bitton (BRO HA/B/18 and 5)
- Thomas Goldney's account book (WRO 473/295) contains the following references where Charles Palmer is named as the individual to whom Coalbrookdale materials are to be delivered
  – November 1757 where Palmer has ordered 7" pit barrels on behalf of Chas Bragge
  – August 1765, one hot well pan (no further details)
  – March 1766, where Palmer delivers screwbolts to the Warmley Company that Jarrit Smith & Co. has to spare (implying he works regularly for both parties)
  – September 1767, 43 boilerplates for the BW (assumed to be Warmley Brassworks) Company
  – 1766 105 Boiler Plates for WM Stones as Gilpin's letter of December 18th
  – December 1768, 49 boilerplates (no further details)
- Charles Palmer provides Jarrit Smith with a valuation of the Warmley companies engine cylinder on 7/5/1772 (BRO AC/AS/93)
- Charles Palmer's Valuation dated 19th January 1779 of the "utensils of the Fire Engine at the New Level Coal Works" (Staple Hill) (GA D421/E21)
- Agreement dated 12th June 1789 between Thomas Palmer and Robert Bond and the representatives of the LoW to construct the Serridge engine. (BRO AC/AS/97/9)
- Taking down the engine at Hanham and re-erecting for Thomas Haynes and Co. at Cowhorn Hill between July 1793 and February 1795. (BRO HA/B/5).

Note that it is an assumption on the author's part that the Palmers named above are related, there is no documentary evidence for this.

Appendix 3
OTHER ACCOUNTS OF NEWCOMEN ENGINE COSTS

Good accounts of component inventories and engine construction costs (as distinct from operating costs) can be found in the following volumes of the *Transaction* of the Newcomen Society:

A. Clayton, 'The Newcomen-Type Engine at Elsecar West Riding'. Vol. 35, 1962 pp 97-108.

J. S. Allen, 'The 1715 and other Newcomen Engines At Whitehaven, Cumberland', Vol. 45, 1972, pp 237-268.

J. S. Allen and J. Elton, 'Edward Short and the 1714 Newcomen Engine at Bilston Staffs', Vol 74B, 2004, pp 281-291.

J. S. Allen, 'The 1712 and other Newcomen Engines of the Earls of Dudley', Vol. 37, 1964,pp 57-82.

PLAN

OF THE PARISH AND

MANOR
of
WESTERLEIGH

IN THE COUNTY OF

GLOCESTER

Surveyd by R Hall 1772 Delineated by J. Sturge 1786.

Coal-Pit   Heath

Ivory Hill

54

INDEX

Entries in *italics* refer to illustrations

People and Organisations

Angerstein, R.R, 29, 36, 42, and *passim*
Ashton Vale Coal & Iron Company, 18, 50
Allen, J.S., 11, 52, 53
Anderson, W.T., 3, *17, 42*
Arthers, Nathaniel, 8, 9, 16, and *passim*
Astry, Samuel, *7,13,*14

Ball, Giles, 28
Bantock, Anton, 45, 51
Barton, D.B., 42
Beaufort, Duke of, 52
Beard, Eustace, 35, 37
Belford, Paul, 42
Berg, Peter,1, *36, 50*
        Torsten and Peter 42, 52
Berkeley Family, 45
Bertram, William, 29
Black Country Museum, 23, 48
Bragge, Charles, 7, 52
Bristol Ironworks, 35
Bristol Records Office, 2, *58,* and *passim*
Bond, Robert, 46, 51, 53
Boulton and Watt, 48, 50
Bowen, William, 50
Bush Mr, 18
Butter, Benjamin, 29

Carron Company, 35
Chatwin, A., 42
Chelsea Waterworks, 11, 31, 38, and *passim*
Clayton, A., 53
Coal Authority, 11, 46, 51
Colston, 7, 27, 45
Cook, Timothy, 29
Cornwell, J., 51
Cowles, Edward, 28, 30
Cranstone, David, 2, 42, 52
Cuming, Sir Alexander, 7
Curr, John, 13, 16, 23, and *passim*

Darby, Abraham, 35, 42
Dartmouth Museum, 18
Deane, Thomas, 51
Diderot, Denis, 32
Dudley, Earls of, 53

Elton, Baron, 29, 30, 42
        Julia, 53
Evans, C., *42,* 52
Evans, Mr, 29, 30

Farmer, John, 28
Fry, Mr, 29

Getty/Getley – see Hillhouse-Getley and Reynolds- Getley
Gilpin, 52
Goldney, Thomas (111), 8, 9, 10, and *passim*
Green, C., 42
Grudgings, 5, 23

Hall, 7, *8,* 10, and *passim*
Hardman, Aaron, 28
Hartley, Dorothy, 50, 51
Hayes, Geoff, 2, 42
Haynes, Thomas, 52, 53
Highnham, Abraham, 31
Hill, Charles, 29
Hills, Thomas, 9, 19, 20, and *passim*
Hillhouse, 29, 40, 41
Hillhouse Getley, 9, 19, 23 and *passim*
Hornblower, Jonathan, 46, 51
Humphreys, Thomas, 10, 46
Huntsman, 29

Ironbridge Gorge Museums Trust, 2, *4,* 11, and *passim*

James, Daniel, 10, 46
Jars, Gabriel, 48
Jenkins, R., 51
Jones, Mr, 29
Jones and Company, 51

Kanesfky J. and Robey J., 11, 51
Kemp, Ken, 2
King, Peter, 42
Kingswood Museum, 51

Lane, James, 28
Lodge Hill Coalworks, 52
London Metropolitan Archives, 11

Malcott, James, 8, 9, 31 and *passim*
Matthews, Messrs/Mr, 19, 29
Middleton, Lord, 5, 7, 8, 11, and *passim*
Mott, R.A., 42
Moone, Joseph, 28
Nash, 35
Neaverson, Peter, 42
Norfolk, Duke of, 13
Northy, Gen'l Sr Edwrd, 11
Nottingham University Archives and Special Collections, 2, 3, 11, *and passim*

O'donaghue, 51

Palmer, Charles, 3, 8, 9 and *passim*
        Thomas, 51, 52, 53
        Arthur, 52
        Marylyn, 42
Penny, J., 42
Pidding, Mr, 29
Ponsford, William, 9, 40
Pope, Ian, 2
Powell, John, 2
Price, Joseph, 28

Raistrick, Dr. A., 6, 11, 42 and *passim*
Reynolds, Getley and Co., 29
Rogers, Ken, 5, 8, *11* and *passim*
Rogers, James, 28
Rolt, L.T.C., 11
Rolt, L.T.C. and Allen,J.S. 48, 51, 52, and *passim*
Rosen, William, 52
Ryden, G., 42, 52

Savery, 11
Science Museum,2, 12, 17 and *passim*
Shallard, 29
Short, Edward, 53
Skinner, William, 28
Smeaton, John, 4
Smith, Jarrit, 7, 13, 27 and *passim*
        John, 45
Smythe, Sir John, 45
        Florence, 45
        Ann, 51
South Gloucestershire Mines Research Group/ SGMRG, 2, 11, *50*
Southway, Matt, 51
Stephenson, George, 3
Stembridge, Peter, 35, 42
Stones, W'M, 52
Sturge, J., 7,

Taylor, Robert 8, 9, 16, and *passim*
Tily, William, 9, 21, 39
Thomson, Francis, 12
Trevethick Society, 19
Tymków,Peter, 2, 42
Victoria and Albert Museum, 18
Vivares, Francois, 19, 24
Watt, James, 27
Wilding, George, 9, 20, 38
Wilkinson, John, 35
Williams, Abraham, 29
Willets, John, 9, 38
Wiltshire and Swindon History Centre, 2, 8, 35
Wise, John, 11, 31, 38 and *passim*

Worcester, Marquis of, 11

Y&DHC, 11

Locations

Ashton Court, 5, 8, 27 and *passim*
Ashton Vale, 50

Badminton, 5, 47, 52
Basque, 29
Bedminster, 46, 51
Bilston, 53
Bitton, 50, 52
Brislington, 3, 11, 50

Caprington Colliery, 2
Central Scotland, 29
Chippenham, 45, 51
Clifton, 11
Cruquius, 10
Cromhall, 50, 51
Coalbrookdale, 7, 8, 15 and *passim*
Coalpit Heath, 3, 4, 5 and *passim*
Cornwall, 6
Cowhorn Hill Colliery, 53

Damsons Bridge, 7
Dartmouth, 18
Dean Lane Colliery, 51
Dudley, 6, 50
Dursley, 45, 51

Elsecar, 2, 34, *38*, and *passim*

Framilode, 9, 20, 29, and *passim*
Frampton Cotterell, 11
Frog Lane Colliery, 6, *11*, 13

Glyn Pits, 42
Griff Colliery, 18
Grimsbury Pit, 51

Hanham, 11, 50, 53
Hawkesbury, 11
Hotwells Road, 29

Ironbridge, 11, 42

Lawfords Gate, 29
Linton, 29

Keynsham, 29
Kingswood, 5,11, 50
Kingswood Common, 52
Lawfords Gate, 19
Lodge Hill, 52

Mangotsfield, 8
Mayshill, 7, 45, 46 and *passim*

Neath, 29
Neath Abbey, 42
New Level Coalworks (Staple Hill), 53
Nibley Coal Works, 7, 50

Oakerthorpe Colliery, 12
O'Donaghue, 51
Old Engine, 13, 46, 47, and passim

Paulton, 50
Pentrich Colliery, 2, 12, *13* and *passim*
Pucklechurch, 50

Radstock, 46
Ram Engine, 13, *14*, 46, and *passim*
Ram Hill, 46
Rangeworthy, 51
Russia, 29

Serridge, 2, 3, 7, and *passim*
Sheffield, 13
Shrewsbury, 35
Siberia, 29
South Liberty Colliery, 18, 33, 50
South Wales, 29
Spain, 29
St. Phillips Plain, 51
Staple Hill, 53
Stapleton Road, 19
Stourbridge/Sturbridge, 21, 29, 30
Sweden, 29

Trowell Field Colliery, 7

Walker Colliery, 48
Warmley, 7, 50
Wednesbury, 9, 38
Westerleigh, 5, 7, 8 and *passim*
Whitehaven, 53
Wollaton, 7, 27

Yate, 50
Yate Heath, 51